A **Del** of a **Life**

DAVID JASON

A Del of a Life

DAVID JASON

LESSONS I'VE LEARNED

CENTURY

1 3 5 7 9 10 8 6 4 2

Century
20 Vauxhall Bridge Road
London SW1V 2SA

Century is part of the Penguin Random House group of companies
whose addresses can be found at global.penguinrandomhouse.com.

Penguin
Random House
UK

First published by Century in 2020

www.penguin.co.uk

A CIP catalogue record for this book is available from the British Library.

Hardback ISBN 9781529125115
Trade Paperback ISBN 9781529125122

Typeset in 13.25/17.5 pt Goudy
by Integra Software Services Pvt. Ltd, Pondicherry

Printed and bound in Great Britain by Clays Ltd, Elcograf S.p.A.

Penguin Random House is committed to a sustainable future for
our business, our readers and our planet. This book is made from
Forest Stewardship Council® certified paper.

MIX
Paper from
responsible sources
FSC
www.fsc.org   FSC® C018179

*This book is dedicated to all my fellow actors who have
helped me along my journey. Thank you*

CONTENTS

INTRODUCTION

'The unexamined life is not worth living.' Socrates

'Get in, get out, don't look back – that's my motto.' Derek
Trotter

February 2nd 2020. On the face of it, it was just another
day. The sun rose in the east, as it tends to when it gets
it right. Birds awakened from their slumbers to herald the
dawn in all its dewy newness. And whistling milkmen began
their rounds – at least in places where they still have milkmen, and in places where those milkmen still whistle.

Meanwhile, at my humble home in the heart of Buckinghamshire, the world stirred as it always does. Horses shook
themselves and whinnied restlessly in the stables, maids
began their tireless labours in the scullery, and the Highland bagpipe player employed to rouse me daily from
beneath my bedroom window completed his performance
and departed on foot across the West Lawn, bound, no
doubt, for his next gig, at Windsor Castle.

As ever, I eased my noble yet surprisingly flexible figure from beneath the counterpane and rose to don the silk dressing gown laid out for me by Strobes, my wrinkled retainer, who, having parted the bedroom curtains, drawn a bath and squeezed the toothpaste onto my brush in anticipation of my morning ablutions, had now gone downstairs to iron my newspaper. In due course, I would follow him down to the breakfast room, help myself to my usual serving of kedgeree from the heated silver salver on the rosewood sideboard, and then settle down to peruse my schedule for the morning.

Just your typical day, then, in the life of your typical knight of the realm and multi-award-winning television actor, namely myself.

Except for one detail: it was my birthday.

Now, if truth be told, I have never been all that fussed about birthdays. I can take them or leave them. And mostly, as time has gone on, I've found myself more inclined to leave them than to take them. But this one was going to be a little harder to ignore. It was one of the so-called big ones. One of the round-numbered ones. It was the day I turned . . .

You know what? I'm actually a little reluctant to write the number down. I find it almost unthinkable that my name and a figure this large belong in the same sentence.

However, needs must.

February 2nd 2020 was my eightieth birthday.

Eighty! I know! How did that happen? I'm not sure that Shakespeare's seven ages of man even go up this far, do they?

I don't mind admitting, I have quite a lot of trouble with the idea of getting old. I know it happens to people – I see it all the time. But surely it's not going to happen to me, is it? In my head, I'm still more or less that bloke you see fooling around in old episodes of *Only Fools and Horses*. When I look in the mirror, I see a twenty-year-old staring out from the body of a senior citizen. How does that work? Young at heart, I suppose you would say, although I can't deny that, in physical terms, my heart is exactly the same age as the rest of me.

Nevertheless, if anyone even mentions the subject of old age in my vicinity, I reflexively go straight into the character – the thin, wavering voice and distant expression – of Blanco, the old lag that I played in the prison comedy *Porridge*. Blanco was the seemingly innocent 'lifer' carefully protected by Ronnie Barker's Fletcher and whom I originally portrayed (and here's a grimly ironic thought, in the present circumstance) at the tender age of thirty.

Comical elderliness? That was one of my earliest calling cards as an actor, right from the first time, in 1969, that Ronnie B asked me to play Dithers, the spectacularly desiccated yet somehow still upright hundred-year-old gardener that Ronnie created for *Hark at Barker* and later for *His Lordship Entertains*. Oh how easily the humiliations of age

3

lent themselves to those slapstick gags! And how we chortled at the terrible varicose veins which were painted on Dithers' legs and which became visible as he disappeared unsteadily up a step ladder in a nightgown! I was twenty-nine when we filmed that sequence. I'm not sure that Jo Tewson ever fully recovered from that scene, as she was holding the steps for Dithers and, as he descended, the nightshirt slowly covered her head and shoulders. Heaven forgive me.

And now I'm eighty. I have outlived Blanco – although not yet Dithers. I'm still working on that.

And I'm not going to complain about it, either. Here's an important truth: getting older most certainly has its downsides. But it still beats the alternative, every time.

Also, as it turned out, I discovered that I was in some extremely good company as a novice octogenarian. Also facing an eightieth birthday at some stage in 2020 were Al Pacino, Tom Jones, Ringo Starr, Raquel Welch and the Battle of Britain. Now, what a dinner party that would be.

Oh, and it was heartening to discover that Batman is even older than me. He came into the world in 1939, making him a sprightly eighty-one. You would never know it to look at him, would you? He's kept himself in pretty decent trim down the years. An example to us all.

I played the part of Batman once, you know. It was in a certain sitcom, and it caused a bit of a stir. But we'll get to that later in these pages.

Eighty though? Look, if it's good enough for Tom Jones and Raquel Welch, it's good enough for me. And furthermore, as I arrived at this distinguished age, it struck me that it would be a perfect moment to take stock – to pause before stepping out into my ninth decade, look back across the journey of my life so far and recount some of the lessons that I've learned along the way.

I've had a long and eventful career – and am still having one, in fact. I've been fortunate enough to be a part of some very successful television shows and even to make a few bits of television history. Along the way I've been given all sorts of advice and learned huge amounts from some great and enormously talented people I've been lucky to work with. I've also learned a lot from some extraordinary characters I've been blessed to play. And I've worked a few things out for myself as well.

All in all, the lessons have been plentiful. Lessons about working; lessons about ambition; lessons about rejection; lessons about success and failure; lessons about fortune and adversity; lessons about friendship; lessons about falling through bar-flaps … It occurred to me that maybe this would be a very good time to pass those life lessons on – before I put them down somewhere and can't remember where I put them.

Those lessons are the substance of this volume. Think of it, if you will, as a summary of what I've learned these four-score years – a review of my life, issuing in a collection of accumulated wisdom, and a compendium of reflections, offered to you from the vantage point afforded me by my extremely impressive maturity.

It's an attempt, I suppose, to find the middle ground somewhere between Socrates and Derek Trotter, with whose famous words this introduction began. (We'll have cause, I'm sure, to seek enlightenment from both those great philosophical thinkers in the ensuing pages, although probably from Derek Trotter more often than from Socrates, if I'm being honest.)

With any luck, some of these thoughts and observations, based on circumstances in which I have found myself, will chime with episodes and challenges you have faced, or are facing, in your own life. And if they don't ... well, hopefully, at the very least you'll get to have a good old laugh at my expense.

I should say straight away that my ninth decade didn't get off to the best of starts. Barely had the birthday cards come down off the mantelpiece than an unprecedented global health crisis was breaking out. Suddenly something called the coronavirus showed up, and we were all obliged to put our lives on hold and go into lockdown for a while. It was a frightening and uncertain period for everybody, for all manner of reasons, and it's still by no means over as I write.

Speaking personally, it was a period when I found myself facing one of my gravest fears, and possibly the thing that haunts all actors, no matter who they are: having no work to do. My essential philosophy all this time, as we'll see, has been to work as hard as I can at every decent opportunity that's been given to me. All of a sudden, though, the entire country froze up and working was no longer an option. Everything in the diary was wiped, and I was actually obliged to sit still for five minutes – in fact, for an awful lot longer than five minutes. All of that was a lesson in itself, and I'll recount that here.

I'll also recall my first tentative return to work under the conditions of 'the new normal' – to present, as it so happened, a programme about my contemporary, the Battle of Britain. That's a documentary that I am very proud to have helped put on the air.

But, before we get to that, by way of an opener, and to set the tone for much of what follows, let me offer you a story with, I think, a strong moral attached to it. It's the story of a pot plant of my acquaintance.

No, seriously. Bear with me.

There are, of course, no horses, stables, sculleries, maids or Highland pipers at my Buckinghamshire home. But not far from me as I write, out in the yard in a giant tub, is a tall, stout grapefruit tree. Now, I've known that grapefruit tree since it was a pip – indeed, since it was a pip in my very own breakfast. To look at it sitting there, all bushy and green, you would never know that it once tried to kill me.

But, to set the scene, I need to take you back to the early seventies – the time of my glory years in the pulsing

West End of London. This was when I had just landed the plum role of Brian Runnicles, taking over from Michael Crawford, in the massively successful farce *No Sex Please, We're British* at the Strand Theatre. Up until then, as a jobbing rep actor with barely two pennies to rub together, I had been living in a one-bedroom flat above my sister-in-law's hairdressing salon, 'Joy's', in Thornton Heath in deepest south London. That flat was fantastically handy if I needed a perm, but less handy if I needed to be at work in the centre of the city which, with my career finally beginning to take off, I increasingly needed to be. A lot of my work at that time was in central London recording studios, doing voice-overs and providing those rich, fruity tones you hear on all those commercials that are so necessary but so irritating and disruptive of one's viewing pleasure.

But then I lucked out. Jo Tewson, the victim of the traumatic nightshirt episode, happened to mention one day that she was about to move out of a rent-controlled flat where she had been living, in a Peabody Estate building just north of Oxford Street. Would I be interested in taking it over? Would I ever. No disrespect to Thornton Heath, but that flat in Newman Street put me at the beating heart of the metropolitan action. A short step north: the One Tun pub in Goodge Street, a notorious watering hole for actors and other reprobates. A short step south: Soho, Seven Dials and the theatres. I could walk to work, and always did.

My new bachelor pad was well-positioned, but it certainly wasn't spacious. The kitchen, in particular, was a poor choice of place to go if you had a cat to swing. I remember, in what was, for me, a brave early stab at sophisticated behaviour, inviting Simon Williams, who was in *No Sex Please*, and his wife Belinda Carroll to 'dinner at my place'. I roasted a chicken. The table in that cramped kitchen was basically a pine plank screwed against the wall with angle brackets and boned up by sandpaper and elbow grease. Those days I spent in the building trade didn't go to waste. Anyway, it meant the three of us had to sit in a row, balancing our plates on this narrow surface and staring at the wall. Which must have seemed a little odd to my guests, though they were nice enough not to mention it.

Anyhow, in another stab at sophistication, I had taken during this period to eating grapefruit for breakfast. It's hard now to relate quite how much of an exotic move that was at the time. The great English fry-up was in retreat, or certainly among a certain class of breakfast consumer. People were talking up the health-giving value of starting your day with a lump of citrus fruit, and smiling bravely while plunging teaspoons into the segmented flesh of halved grapefruits. Never mind that an imported grapefruit could be both rock solid and punishingly sour. And never mind, either, that if you dug your spoon in at the wrong angle, a fine jet of grapefruit juice would arch directly into your eye and blind you for the rest of the day.

And that's before we even mention the pips. It was a pip that nearly did for me. I was gamely chipping away with the spoon one morning, and no doubt eagerly enjoying my breakfast's invigorating bitterness, when a pip got stuck in my throat. There ensued a coughing fit so violent and protracted that it's a wonder both of my eyes remained in my head at the end of it.

At least the pip was no longer in my throat, though. It was now on the kitchen table in front of me. Still breathing heavily, I looked down at it. The pip looked back up at me. Something about its expression seemed to plead for forgiveness. I looked at it long and hard. It looked at me long and hard. Well, I suppose it was one of those mornings ... I had nothing planned, at least until the evening, when I would be tripping my way down Newman Street, across Soho Square, down to Garrick Street and on to the Strand Theatre. Meanwhile, across the top of Newman Street, just off Goodge Street, was a little road called Goodge Place where a small builders' merchants sat in the corner of what used to be a stable yard. It was a tiny, family-run business, absolutely nothing like the giants we have today, and, indeed, it was the place where I had got the wood for the kitchen table that so impressed my co-stars, Simon and Belinda. It was also the place I used to go to fetch paraffin for my heater, which I kept in the hall and which acted as central heating on those cold, winter days. When I returned after the show on a winter's night, the hall would be warm as toast and, by clever opening and closing of doors, I could get each room to warm up to just below freezing.

Anyway, it was to that little builders' merchants that I took myself that morning to purchase a small bag of compost and a plastic pot. I then carried those items back up the four flights of stairs to the flat where I filled the pot with soil and, pausing only to forgive it for trying to throttle me, planted the pip.

The back of the flat looked out onto a well in the block, which was quite gloomy but had been white-tiled to make it a bit lighter. It seemed unlikely that I would be able to get anything to grow out there, but it was the best bet that I had, so I gave it a go. I stood the pot out on the kitchen windowsill and began watering it diligently.

I didn't give it much hope, but one morning, some weeks later, I looked out and a tiny bud had emerged from the soil. Amazing: this thing was alive. I was genuinely moved. It was a tribute to the powers of nature, and also to the power of London tap water. I continued to water it, and it continued to grow. Initially a rather unpromising-looking sapling, it was soon something more clearly definable as a 'plant'.

Sometimes in the ensuing years, work took me away for whole weeks at a time, doing summer seasons. At such times, I would ask Micky and Angie, my good friends and neighbours across the hall, to water my plant for me. They would have to unlock the flat and go in just to tend to this one small pot out on the sill, which must have seemed like a lot of effort for not very much. But I didn't care. I was now hooked on horticulture. And the grapefruit stayed alive. There were only a couple of occasions when I came home and found it gasping for water and apparently on the verge of quitting on me. But bless its cotton socks, it always recovered and stuck with the programme.

In due course, it was big enough that I had to re-pot it. Soon after that, it was big enough that I had to attach a piece of wire around the pot to stop it dropping off the windowsill and into the well and braining someone. Obviously the safety of my fellow tenants was my first concern here. Actually, it probably wasn't. My first concern was the safety of the plant.

Eventually, whole years later, when I moved out of London, it came with me. When I moved again, it came, too. Once – just once – it tried to fruit. There were three little grapefruits on it, each the size of a pea. I was incredibly proud. About a week later, they all fell off.

Someone suggested keeping it indoors in a more constantly warm environment to see if it could be induced to fruit again. The plant rebelled against its domestication by developing some kind of leaf infestation. I treated it for the rot and stood it outside again.

And now here it is, still with me half a century later, in its huge container, standing tall with a trunk which is about four inches in diameter. It spends every winter in the summerhouse, because a sharp frost would probably do for it, even now. And then in the summer, I drag it out into the yard, practically doing myself a mischief every time because it's so heavy. It tried to kill me then, and, in its own sweet way, it's still trying to kill me now. Nevertheless, in some strange way, I love that plant and I still care for it. I suppose, in return, it reminds me of that very particular part of my journey – those days in London.

So what's the moral of this story? The moral of this story is that if you take an unpromising little seed and patiently water it, then eventually it will get so big that you'll put your back out trying to drag the damn thing into the daylight.

At least, that's one way of expressing the moral. But you could also say that what this grapefruit tree of mine demonstrates is that, if you very carefully nurture something, and stick at it determinedly, you may be surprised by the scale of what you create. Overwhelmed by it, even.

There's a pretty strong parallel with my life story here. But let's find out.

CHAPTER ONE

On matters medical and constitutional

'I mean, look at him. His brain went years ago. Now his legs have gone. There's only the middle bit of him left.' Derek Trotter, discussing Grandad

As a multi-award-winning television actor and knight of the realm who now finds himself sashaying down the catwalk of his ninth decade, I am often asked – by magazines and television programmes mainly, but sometimes also by overawed strangers in the street who grab me by the arm – to share the secrets of my longevity.

'So lithe,' they say. 'So spry and sparkling. So uncannily youthful. How on earth do you do it?'

Well, what can I tell you? An hour of tai chi first thing in the morning; an intense work-out with my personal trainer, mostly concentrating on squats and lunges in order to fire the glutes and maintain that all-important core strength; a bowl of steamed kale and a handful of almonds for lunch;

then two hours of yoga in the afternoon followed by an ice bath – this is a routine which I'm sure would work miracles for anyone of any age, although I can't be entirely sure because I haven't myself adopted any aspect of it at any point.

To what, then, can I genuinely attribute the robustness of my constitution at this impressively late stage of the game? Fluke, I fear. The great good fortune of one's genes. Along, I suppose, with a general avoidance, by and large, down the years, of life-endangering excess, unless you count operating a Flymo (see later).

The lesson being: everything in moderation, including moderation.

Or, as the other old but undimmed piece of wisdom has it: try everything once, with the exception of Morris dancing and incest. Consequently, at the time of writing I am delighted and relieved to be able to report that I don't yet match Del's somewhat uncharitable verdict on the state of Grandad, above.

Incidentally, I can't think about those typically great John Sullivan lines without affectionately remembering how the late Lennard Pearce, who played Grandad in *Only Fools*, would use his relatively advanced years to excuse all manner of misdemeanours on his part, whether it was fluffing a line or jumping the queue for tea in the canteen. 'I'm old,' he would say. 'I'm allowed.'

Now, that's a philosophy which, for some reason, I increasingly find myself inclined to stand by. You're old – you're allowed.

But it's clear that I am lucky. Every year I have to go for the standard aviation medical in order to keep myself qualified as a helicopter pilot. And every time, I'm nervous as a kitten beforehand because I'm worried that this will be the year the doctor consults his charts, looks at me with a sympathetically pained expression and says, 'Have you ever considered golf?' Flying is one of my greatest passions, and the best thing outside of acting that I ever learned to do, and I'm going to be extremely upset if the time comes that I have to leave it behind.

Up to now, though (and here you must imagine me reaching for the nearest wooden surface), I've come through those aviation medicals with no problem. You could even say I've flown through them. And statistics would encouragingly suggest that I've got plenty of helicopter hours left in me. According to Guinness World Records, the oldest solo pilot helicopter flight was conducted by a gentleman named David Marks, who was a mere eighty-seven years and forty days old when he took an Enstrom F28 from Northampton Sywell Airfield to Fenland Airfield in September 2017. Good work. I would love to take that record away from him one day. It's a target to aim for.

Anyway, according to the most recent of those medicals my constitution remains blessedly sound, here in the summer of 2020. My hearing and my eyesight both appear to be in decent fettle and my blood pressure is where it ought to be. In addition to that, I can also confirm that I have my own teeth – and frankly, at this stage, I wouldn't be all that keen on having anyone else's. And I still appear to be playing with a more or less full complement of marbles, a privilege which none of us can take for granted and for which I thank my lucky stars every day.

I guess the decision to quit smoking a while ago was probably a good one. As Dr Shaheed (played by Josephine Welcome) once asked Del, in an episode of *Only Fools* that saw him rather reluctantly going to get some stomach pains checked out:

'Do you smoke, Mr Trotter?'

And as Del replied:

'Not just now, thank you, doctor.'

I don't smoke, but I certainly did, and for a long time. I quit when I was sixty, in fact, when my wife Gill and I decided we were going to have a baby. Had I come to fatherhood earlier, maybe I wouldn't have smoked for so long, but that was not how it panned out.

I enjoyed smoking while I did it but, my word, what an extraordinary habit it was, really. The more I think about it, the less sense it made. It wasn't just a drain on my financial resources during a period (the late 1950s and the 1960s) when I could ill afford it, it was also spectacularly bad for you – although, in fairness, nobody really told us that, back in the day. But over and above those considerations, it was also, when looked at in the cold light of day, just a plainly ridiculous thing to be getting up to.

The fundamental absurdity of smoking has never been better exposed and exploited for laughs than by the American comic genius Bob Newhart (aged ninety when I wrote this, by the way, and still performing). Newhart wrote a sketch called 'Introducing Tobacco to Civilisation', where he set himself up as the head of the West India Company taking a call from Sir Walter Raleigh, at some unspecified point in the late sixteenth century, about this new tobacco thing that Raleigh seems to have discovered in the West Indies, and responding with increasing disbelief and bemusement, which shades eventually into outright mockery.

'It's a kind of leaf ... and you bought eighty tons of it ... Walt, don't tell me: you stick it in your ear, right? ... Oh, between your lips ... Then what do you do, Walt? ... You set fire to it? ... You see, Walt, we've been a little worried about you, you know, ever since you put your cape down over that mud.'

That sketch was on Newhart's 1960 album, *The Button-Down Mind of Bob Newhart*, which was an enormous hit, as comedy albums could be in those days, both in the US and in the UK. It beat Frank Sinatra to the Grammy for Best Album that year, which just about sums it up. I bought and devoured that record. I thought it was the funniest thing I had ever heard – verbal humour and comic timing on another level. I laughed at that tobacco sketch then, and I laugh at it now. It was the perfect skewering of a habit which, at the time, we all took for granted.

Yet I carried on smoking, of course.

The thing was, smoking looked so great when people did it in the movies. That was where me and my teenage chums first got the idea that Sir Walter Raleigh was on to something. Humphrey Bogart could talk and drive while smoking and the cigarette would never leave his lips. That seemed like a rare kind of magic to us, and a skill very much to be emulated at the earliest possibility. Not to mention the fact that men who smoked in films seemed very often to end up with women, who also smoked. In our impressionable teenage minds, cigarettes were a symbol of the great but thus far inaccessible pleasures of adulthood. Indeed, they were more than that: they were an actual ticket to those pleasures.

Our curiosity was bound to overcome us eventually. When I was about fourteen, a gang of us used to go ice skating at the rink in Church End, Finchley. That venue boasted, in a conveniently discreet location, a cigarette vending machine. None of us in my bunch had the money with which to buy cigarettes, but we did have the entrepreneurial foresight to realise that, with a little jiggery and a little pokery, that particular machine, which must have had a few screws loose here and there, could be made to yield its desirable contents for the price of exactly no money at all.

And as my father used to say: 'What costs ya nuffink can't be dear.'

When nobody was looking, we duly jiggered and poked, and bingo: not just one but several packets dropped out of the machinery, a veritable tobacco jackpot. We were so happy: now we could become smokers. For free!

We rushed back to our favoured hang-out – the alley by the Finchley Postal Sorting Office at the bottom of Lodge Lane – in a hurry to light up and instantly become grown-ups.

It's a shame the next few moments weren't captured on film. Cigarettes were solemnly handed around. I believe the brand was Capstan Full Strength – and maybe the clue was in the name. Someone had some matches. We all lit up and sucked, drawing the warm smoke into our lungs for the first time. Alas, our lungs were less sure about the wisdom of this than we were and, in unison, they promptly shoved the smoke back out again. Lodge Lane probably hadn't witnessed an explosion like it since that bomb dropped. Every one of us instantly choked in a cloud of exhalation. I personally endured a coughing fit the scale of which I wouldn't know again until all those years later when I swallowed the grapefruit pip. I believe at least one among our number coughed so hard that he was actually sick. That might have been me, actually.

You might think the glamour would have gone out of the game at that point. Not a bit of it. We might have been foolish, but we were persistent. And persistence is, in the end, what separates the merely foolish among us from the, er … persistently foolish. Far from renouncing smoking as a bad idea there and then, we simply decided that, like any skill that was worth acquiring, it was obviously going to need practice. And practice we did, with the result that we were all soon – if you don't mind me saying – rather good at it.

Incidentally, here's a coincidence. Exactly at this time, in the mid-1950s, in a drive to encourage more women to smoke their products, Capstan were using the extremely popular singer and actor Evelyn Laye in their advertising. There was a wonderful ad featuring a picture of Evelyn looking impeccably glamorous with a fag on, and the following lines of copy: 'If you were Evelyn Laye – sweet-singing star of *Wedding in Paris* – and you had a few minutes' interval between scenes, what would you do?'

Well, what do you think? Have a glass of water? A throat lozenge? A quick rub-down with a cold flannel? Wrong.

'Have a CAPSTAN – they're made to make friends.'

Or made to make friends sick, in my case. But the reason I mention this is because about twenty years after this experimental episode in the alley, I would be acting with Evelyn Laye on the West End stage in *No Sex Please*. And if you had told me that while I was coughing up my teenage guts at the bottom of Lodge Lane that evening, I probably would have laughed so hard at the absurdity of the notion that I would have ended up being sick all over again.

Anyway, I moved on to Silk Cut eventually – probably between five and ten a day, always in the evenings. I wasn't a particularly heavy smoker, then – or it didn't seem so, comparatively. I was never one of those smokers who fumbled blearily for the packet on the bedside table in the morning, or who really had to worry if they ever ran out. But I was consistent, and I stuck with it – or got stuck with it, depending how you want to look at it.

Of course, it was so much easier to be a smoker in those days. There was nowhere you couldn't do it: buses, trains, pubs, rehearsal rooms, dressing rooms, theatres – down in the London Underground, even. Most amazing of all, in retrospect, was the smoking section in aeroplanes – two or three rows at the back of the plane, reserved for us leaf-burners, because obviously there was no way the smoke would drift forward from there and affect the experience of the travellers in the rest of the cabin. Again, one's jaw drops to reflect on how perfectly reasonable this felt at the time.

Nowadays, smoking seems mostly to be done outside office blocks, by slightly guilty-looking people in little clusters or, even more poignantly, on their own, furtively grabbing a fag and braving the elements to do so. When I see them, I always feel a twinge of solidarity (once a smoker, always a smoker, at least in spirit, surely) but also a touch of sadness. Needs must, of course, but it always seems a bit forlorn to me. Has smoking's once great promise come to this? It didn't look like that when Humphrey Bogart did it.

I've been lightly bragging about my durability here, but of course I'm as subject as anyone else to what I have come to think of as 'ageing primate syndrome'. And what extraordinary effects that syndrome can have upon the human frame. The automatic extension in later years of the male stomach, for instance, is, whatever else you want to say about it, truly one of the great wonders of biology. You don't need to apply for planning permission, or anything. It just happens, and where once you may have prided yourself on your washboard abs, the next thing you know you're looking down at the laundry basket.

And what goes on with earlobes, too? Boy, do earlobes enjoy themselves during the autumn of your years. You barely think about them for the majority of your life, and then suddenly they decide to deflate like old car tyres and set off in the direction of the floor as if in tribute to Disney's Pluto.

And then there's your hair. Or rather, and then there are the places where your hair used to be. Not unlike my life insurance policy, my hair started to offer diminishing coverage as I reached my forties. 'Typical male-pattern baldness' was the term for it – or, as I preferred to express it at the time: 'Typical! Male-pattern baldness!'

One day, all was thick and lustrous back there, and the next I noticed that my crown was privately auditioning for a role in a drama about monks. That was unhelpful of it – especially as the rest of me had just been asked to resume the role of Granville the shop-lad, opposite Ronnie Barker's grouchy shop-keeper Arkwright, in *Open All Hours*.

More than five years separated series one of that show from series two – an unusual gap in the life of a comedy, and, indeed, in the meantime we had all come to assume the show was dead and buried. The BBC had taken the decision to put that first series out on BBC2, much to the disappointment of all of us who had worked on it. BBC2 was where the off-beat, the irregular, the non-mainstream programmes were given their home, and I think all of us had thought that *Open All Hours* was a show with really broad appeal, strong enough to duke it out with the kinds of programme that were trusted to draw bigger audiences on BBC1.

Yet, somewhere within the corporation's upper echelons, the view had taken hold that this was a 'gentle comedy'. Ronnie Barker absolutely hated that term. He would point out that when people describe a comedy as 'gentle', what they generally mean is that they don't think it's very funny. It's the same when people tell you that something you were in 'made me smile'. Lovely compliment and everything, and you can never have too many. But really? Only smile? It was meant to make you laugh ...

Anyway, series one of *Open All Hours* duly went out on BBC2 and, in what was basically a self-fulfilling prophecy, it attracted only minor interest and generated unspectacular audiences. I was very glum about that at the time. It was yet another occasion (and trust me, there were a lot of these along the way) when I had found myself in a show that I was really convinced was going to do well, garner vast amounts of critical acclaim and finally thrust my television star firmly into the firmament. But no. Instead of a 'bang', I heard a 'phut'.

Fully five years later, that first series got repeated – this time on BBC1, which should have been its home all along. And it wouldn't have happened if Ronnie Barker and Ronnie Corbett hadn't decided to take themselves off to Australia for a year. This was a period of history when UK tax was eye-wateringly high. Eighty-three per cent was the top rate, going into 1979, and even the basic rate was a stiff 33 per cent. Dick Clement and Ian La Frenais, the writing team behind *Porridge*, had apparently alerted Ronnie B to the perfectly legal loophole wherein you could ease your tax burden by the simple expedient of going abroad for a year. The Ronnies thought about this and decided that Australia looked nice. Ronnie B used to laugh about the tax expert that he and Ronnie Corbett consulted about this, who simply said to them, 'I wish I was coming with you.' In 1979, the Ronnies packed up their families and went to live in Sydney.

That left the BBC staring into a big void where two of its most popular and most prolific comic artists had been. One of the remedies was to plug the gap with a repeat screening of *Open All Hours*, but this time on BBC1

– where, what do you know? People seemed to really like it and started showing up for it in big numbers. Roy Clarke was commissioned to write another series, and when Ronnie B returned from Australia, the team got back together again for what felt more like a revival than a continuation of the job.

By this time, my hair had had four years in which to start turning grey at the temples and, in the case of that vulnerable area at the back of my head, to vacate the premises completely. I'd been acting younger than my years when I played Granville in the first place. He was meant to be about thirty, and I was thirty-five the first time, and what felt like the creakingly ancient age of forty now. Thank heavens, then, for the magic of showbusiness, where you are only ever really as old as the make-up department makes you look. There was nothing that couldn't be lastingly remedied by the application of a small hairpiece, clipped to the affected area, and some dye. Three further series ensued, and nobody was any the wiser, really. Well, except, some years later, for my daughter Sophie, who was quick to twig that something was up. When she was little she used to refer to it as 'that programme when Daddy had black hair'.

By then it was 1981 and I had just started working on another comedy show whose first series met with a mostly indifferent reception, and whose future at first didn't look all that bright. It was about a pair of wheeler-dealers living in a tower block in Peckham. I would have to wait and see how that went.

> The lesson being: you may hear many phuts before you hear a bang. But nothing beats the sound of a bang after a succession of phuts.

It was ageing primate syndrome, I guess, that left me needing a canalicular bypass. Stay with me: it's not quite as painful it sounds. The canal in question was in my eye, where a little blockage had started causing it to get a bit weepy from time to time. You can sort that out pretty straightforwardly by having Jones tubes inserted. Simple but brilliant devices, Jones tubes are named after their inventor, Lester Jones, who, with a name like that, would probably have done quite well as a jazz trumpeter if the ophthalmology hadn't worked out. The procedure is very straightforward and is called a conjunctivodacryocystorhinostomy.

Try saying that with a mouthful of Werther's Originals. Actually, try saying that while someone is poking around in your tear duct with a Jones tube. If you had asked me a couple of years ago what a dacryocystorhinostomy was, I'd have said it had probably died out with all the other dinosaurs. But you live and learn.

Jones tubes do a very good job, but they have one drawback, which is that they tend to come out and you lose them, and then you have to go back and have them replaced. The first time I had mine inserted, I asked the specialist, 'How do they stay in?' Because they were just tiny tubes, completely smooth. There didn't seem to be anything to hold them in position.

I couldn't help myself. The ghost of my early years as a jobbing electrician who worked on building sites awoke, as it still does surprisingly often, and I found myself standing there, hands on hips and an appraising expression on my face, saying, 'You know what? You want to get a flange on that, mate.'

I'm sure the specialist thought: yes, well, thank you for your brilliant medical input, and the next time we're designing these things, we'll contact you if we feel we need to.

But let me tell you something: two years later, I was back in the surgery for a re-fit and the doctor was showing me the latest tubes that had just come in, hot out of the factory – and they had flanges on. Flanges in order to hold them in place a bit better.

I hate to say I told you so, but ... I told you so.

I missed a trick there. I should have stuck to my guns when the idea occurred to me and then hopped straight down to the patents office. Never mind Jones tubes, we could be talking about Jason tubes, and I'd be quids in. Opportunity squandered.

Canalicular bypass aside, though, I'm aware that I have been a highly fortunate man. I'll be struggling to regale you otherwise with tales of my times in hospital. I did once upon a time go to A&E after running over my foot with a Flymo, but even mentioning that in this context makes me sound a bit like Del again.

Dr Shaheed: 'Do you have trouble passing water?'

Del: 'I had a dizzy spell going over Tower Bridge once.'

I know I'm lucky in that I've been able to spend nearly my whole working life acting. And acting is many things. It's difficult sometimes. It can involve long hours – and unsociable hours, too. It requires concentration and physical effort. But it's not constantly punishing in the way that so many jobs are – 'proper jobs', some would say, though I wouldn't be among them. I think acting is a proper job. I've certainly always treated it as one, and I'm certain I wouldn't have got as far as an actor if I hadn't. But nobody should pretend that it's punishing in the way that manual labour is punishing.

My first job after I left school at fifteen was at Popes Garage in Finchley. There was a gap along the bottom of the main doors to that workshop through which you could have slid a car-jack and, in the winter, the wind would come whistling right through – most painfully if you happened to be on the concrete floor under a car at the time. When I was setting off on my acting journey, slogging around the provincial theatres in under-par farces, and the breaks weren't coming and I was thinking of throwing it all in, the memory of that draught shooting up the legs of my overalls while engine oil dripped on me from above was one of the things that inspired me to keep at it. I didn't want to go back there if I could avoid it.

I also think of my dad, who spent his working life sloshing about in cold water, as fishmongers are destined to do, and then paid for it later with crippling arthritis. Acting's not like that. It isn't hard labour, however much actors will try to persuade you to the contrary.

The secret of my longevity, then? In as much as I've had any control over it, it's that I ended up doing something I love. Then all you can do is hope the rest of it takes care of itself.

CHAPTER TWO

On humble beginnings and surprising outcomes

'Life must be lived forwards, but it can only be understood backwards.' Søren Kierkegaard

You've got to hand it to the boy Kierkegaard: he was really on to something there. On we drive down time's pot-holed B-road from day to day, having little alternative, there being no reverse gear in the great Austin Allegro of life. But the patterns that might make any sense of it all are only really visible when you pull over, park up for a bit and look back along the road. Nice one, Søren.

By the way, before you commend me on the depth of my reading in nineteenth-century Danish philosophy, my wife Gill found that quotation for me in a John Mortimer novel she was reading. Spared me a few days up a ladder among the book stacks in the Jason Towers library there. Cheating? Maybe. But it doesn't mean those words are any less true.

Now, funnily enough, I realise, looking back, that I've never really been someone who made a habit of … looking back. I've always been a little wary of it. In part, I'm sure that's been to do with protecting myself. Obviously it's nice to remember old times and the great things you got up to and the enjoyment that you had. But then there's the flip-side to that, which is that so many of those great and lovely things have gone and you can't get them back. I find that very hard to deal with, and that's why in my head, when the chance of nostalgia looms, there's very often a voice, not dissimilar to that of an American cop, barking, 'Step away from the photo album!'

When I sat down to write my first book of memoirs in 2013 (still available where good books are sold, dear reader, if you haven't already invested in it), it was genuinely the first time I had thought hard about many of the things I had done and many of the projects I had worked on since the time they actually happened. I resisted writing about my life for a long while, even though people kept telling me to get on with it before my memory turned to flaky pastry.

Although, now I think of it, the memoir of an actor who has forgotten everything and started thinking he was in all sorts of films and shows that he was never a part of sounds like a book I'd be quite keen to read. Maybe next time …

Anyway, my point is, when I did eventually cast an eye back over my life for the purposes of that book, it surprised me how much of it there was. While you're in the middle of cracking on with it, it's easy to lose a sense of how much living you've done.

The lesson being: more things have happened in your life than you have taken the time to notice.

On top of that, from a professional point of view, dwelling overly on the past has tended to worry me. Taking time out to revisit past triumphs has always smacked slightly to me of laurels and resting on them. And taking time out to revisit past disasters is either too funny or too painful, or, worst of all, both those things at the same time. It's important to enjoy your successes to some extent, clearly, else why bother? And it's equally important to learn what you can from your failures. Yet, in the main, from my point of view, the best tactic seemed to be to plough on to the next job and, with any luck, the one after that. Up in the morning, head down, nose to the grindstone and on you go.

I'm still that way, and I suspect it's like that for a lot of actors. It's in the nature of the business. It doesn't matter how successful you are, you're always worried about the next thing and whether or not it might show up. And you're convinced that if too long a period goes by where you're sitting idle, all of that effort you've gone to, to climb the ladder and build some kind of presence for yourself higher up the board, will be as nothing and people will forget who you are. Back down the snake to square one.

Yet even I, for all my insistent onward thrusting (if I may put it that way), have known my contemplative moments – occasions when the velvet cloak of retrospection has descended upon my shoulders (not literally) and I have seen the need to pause and take a backwards glance. Writing that book was obviously one such. So, too, was the prospect of an eightieth birthday, if you can imagine such a thing. One of those will certainly make you stop and think, take it from me. And so, as it happens, will a global pandemic which has closed the world down and left you sat at home, staring at the fireplace. It turns out that the past and all its possible meanings rise unbidden to the mind in such a circumstance.

And have those periods of contemplation brought me to a place of understanding, vis-à-vis my travels through time's gauzy mists? Let me say this: when I look back at the journey my life has taken, I'm struck first and foremost by how hard it is to believe it, let alone understand it.

Consider me in 1960, aged twenty, and at this point known to the world – or rather, not remotely known to the world – as David White. I'm in a pair of dark blue overalls and sitting behind the wheel of a second-hand Standard Companion, which is a kind of boxy estate car, the shape of which simply oozes the staid essence of British motoring in the mid-1950s. I am five foot six, a giddy height to which a growth spurt took me at fourteen. Alas, that's also where the growth spurt left me, and now, at twenty, I am more or less fully resigned to the fact that a further growth spurt won't be happening any time soon.

Alongside me in the passenger seat, and also in overalls, is my friend Bob Bevil, who is not a great deal taller than I am, as it happens. Clearly people were meant to be shorter in those days. Bob and I, having left school after less than distinguished academic careers, have recently completed our apprenticeships with the Electricity Board at Enfield Technical College. And the Electricity Board has equally recently elected, in its wisdom, not to keep either of us on in full-time employment.

Their loss, of course – although, to be fair, Bob and I did spend a lot of our time at Enfield College focused less on the minutiae of electrical theory and more on the minutiae of mucking about. You know the kind of thing: staging pranks involving copper wiring and hammers, using the staple gun to attach fellow apprentices to the floor by their boiler-suits, organising elaborate dramas during lessons in which we all pretended to be prisoners of war – that kind of stuff. Perhaps it's not entirely surprising, then, that when it cast its appraising eye over the graduating class of 1959, the Board chose to release students Bevil and White into the wild, and to deny us access to the steady stream of work that was within the Board's gift.

But were we downcast? Well, yes, actually. It felt like a bit of a thumb in the eye, to be honest. Two years was a long time for anybody to spend on day release at Enfield College, especially when you were going there by bike from Finchley, eight miles away, as I was a lot of the time. And steady work was steady work, as my understandably anxious parents had been pointing out for a couple of years by this point.

On the other hand, both Bob and I now had certificates of qualification, testifying to our competence as electricians. We also had a fair bit of practical experience under our belts, because on the four days of the working week when you weren't attending college, the Board packed you off to jobs on building sites, or sent you to report to one of the Electricity Board Showrooms – a vanished institution now, but a high street fixture then – where you would be sent round the back to make yourself busy mending people's kettles and toasters. You didn't get through all of that without becoming pretty nifty with a soldering iron.

Taking all of this into account, snubbed though we obviously had been, Bob and I decreed that the world of wiring should not have heard the last of us. We set up our own electrical business, BW Installations & Co. Business address? My parents' house in Lodge Lane. Business phone number? My parents' number at Lodge Lane – Hillside 3526.

You answered the phone by stating your local exchange and number in those days. And you did so precisely and clearly, in the voice you kept for best. The phone seemed to demand these high standards, much as it seemed to create untold levels of mystery whenever it rang. 'Who could that be?' someone would always say. 'Who could that possibly be?'

'Well, why not flipping answer it and find out?' one would be tempted to reply these days. But telecommunications, of course, simply don't have the power to astound us as once they did, and back then one merely shared everybody else's profound levels of wonder and bemusement at the miraculous sound of an incoming call. Who could that possibly be, indeed?

Anyway, here we are, then, Bob and me, in 1960, most likely as the consequence of answering a call to Hillside 3526, going about our business in our work car. Loads of tools in the back – and a couple of tools in the front, some might have argued. Perhaps we are on our way to a block of flats to install an intercom system – another technical marvel, fresh on the scene, a magnificent breakthrough and undoubted boon, enabling flat-dwellers to answer the door without clambering all the way down the stairs. This was a golden period for intercom fitters, and Bob and I got a lot of work in that line. So, picture us, if you will, driving round Hyde Park Corner in London, on our way, perhaps, to a flat in Victoria, and heading down Grosvenor Place, with Buckingham Palace on the left.

Now, imagine that, at this exact moment, as the high wall bordering the immense garden of the Royal Family's main London residence passes by the Standard's side window, I am granted by some mysterious force a vision of the future. The vision dances briefly but gloriously in my mind and then, its message from tomorrow imparted, fades as quickly as it came.

At which point, I turn to my fellow electrician and, gesturing to the tall garden wall on our left, say: 'You know what, Bob, I'll be driving in there one day, on the way to collect my knighthood. I now know this for a fact, on account of a vision of the future which was just that second granted to me by a mysterious force which, having imparted its message to me, faded as quickly as it came.'

Frankly, Bob would have fallen out of the passenger door laughing. Not about the idea of me getting a vision of the future; about the idea, far less plausible, of me going to Buckingham Palace to be made a knight. At the very least he would have wondered what I'd been putting in my sandwiches. (Nothing stronger than Cheddar cheese, as a rule.) At that point in my life, it would have seemed an absolutely preposterous notion – to both of us. Not even the stuff of dreams – the stuff of crime. The only way someone like me was getting into Buckingham Palace during an awards ceremony was by going over the wall and getting arrested shortly thereafter.

Things don't really get any more comprehensible if I go back even further in my journey, right to the beginning of the story. Once again, the effect of travelling backwards into the past is to deliver, not so much understanding on my part, as sheer incredulity. Sorry, Søren. Am I doing it wrong or something?

A brief recap, if I may. I arrive at North Middlesex County Hospital in February 1940 and am taken home to 26 Lodge Lane, Finchley, a tiny, three-up three-down house in the middle of a typical north London Victorian terrace. My father, Arthur White, is a fishmonger, initially a porter at Billingsgate market, and then later a worker behind the counter at branches of Mac Fisheries in Camden Town and Golders Green. My mother, Olwen, whose family is Welsh, works as a charwoman for a well-off family in Finchley. She had been their live-in maid until she met my dad and married him.

Bombs drop, on and off, for the next five years. One of my earliest memories is of raising my eyes to the sky and seeing and, more ominously, hearing a doodlebug – a German V-1 flying bomb – passing over our roof. This would be at some point between June and October 1944 when Germany sent more than 9,500 of these terrifying, death-bringing automatons into the skies over south-east England from launch sites on the French coast. When the motor stops, the bomb drops. Accordingly, the thing you hope very fervently not to hear is the sound of the motor stopping.

A census map of Second World War bomb damage shows thirteen bomb strikes of various kinds within a five-block stretch on the Lodge Lane side of Finchley High Road: four on or in the vicinity of Lodge Lane itself, three more one street away at Woodside Park Road, and another one in Percy Road, one street in the other direction. My brother,

41

Arthur, seven years older than me, is evacuated to the countryside for his own safety. I'm too little for that, so I stay in London and stick it out. I become inured, more or less, to the toddler-sized gas mask and the indoor Morrison shelter under which we are strongly advised to crawl in the event of an air-raid siren. (My sister, June, has the sound good sense to give the war a swerve entirely: she comes along seven years after me, in 1947.)

Everything is rationed: meat, butter, cheese, tea, sugar, jam, eggs and even soap. The house has no electricity and no bathroom. It has gas lights, an outside loo, in a lean-to in the yard, and a tin bath hanging on a hook on the back door. Electricity will arrive in a blaze of glory and amid great rejoicings, in the early 1950s, followed shortly after by television. The Priors get a television in 1953, in time for Queen Elizabeth's Coronation. We get ours two years later, in time for *Dixon of Dock Green*, *Life with the Lyons* and *This Is Your Life* (of which more anon).

Before the television comes, though, evenings are spent listening to the radio while my parents take it in turns to read the *Mirror* by the dull light of a gas mantle. The gas lights are lit in the downstairs rooms only. Upstairs in the bedroom I share with Arthur, once he is returned to us from the countryside, there's a candle in a tin holder, but that's only really for when one of us is confined to bed and ill. Most nights we go to bed in the dark. I'll be having my face washed in the kitchen and Arthur, already on his way up, will be calling out through the banisters: 'Is David coming? Hurry up.' Neither of us really likes to be up there in the dark on our own. Indeed, Arthur practically suffocates me one night, crawling into my bed when I'm only just big enough to be using it, and converting me into an improvised security blanket.

Or maybe he was just after a hot water bottle because the house is pretty cold in the main – draughty and heated solely by a small grate in the kitchen and another in the living room. Every few weeks the coalman arrives, wearing a leather skullcap with a long leather flap hanging down his back to rest the sacks on. He'll stomp through the house, a big stocky bloke who seems far too big for the place, and he'll squeeze through the kitchen and go out of the back door to pour his sack into a kind of cupboard in the back yard. That coal will fuel those two fires, both of which are powerful enough to warm any parts of you that are directly facing them, but not, alas, the rest of you, which will remain cold.

On Friday nights my parents go up the road to someone else's house to play cards, taking me with them. Another early memory here: of sitting in that house and beginning to fall asleep to the sound of adult voices ('Jack of Clubs, Queen, King … Anybody got the Ace?'). And then eventually being carried home over the shoulder of my father, with a blanket round me, in that wonderful place in between sleep and wakefulness – out in the open air, but not cold, too far gone to wake up, yet semi-conscious. Something sublime about the security of that feeling. And then being carried upstairs and placed into bed, where the sheets are cold enough to bring you closer to waking, but where you are too tired to let it bother you.

England at this time is quite possibly the most class-bound society in the world (and it probably remains so now, too) and class infuses everything. The *Mirror* is for working-class people like us. Other papers are for nobs, not like us. So many things seem to be this way – books, clothes, where you drink, what you eat, how you speak, the job you do: all of it is either your kind of thing, or not your kind of thing, as if by decree. Aspiration does not really seem to figure in our lives. It doesn't figure at school, where no one seems to be pushing you very hard to be anything other than what you already are; and it doesn't figure at home, either. You are assumed to know your place. Somewhere along the way my father gets offered some kind of managerial role at Mac Fisheries – a promotion. Better pay. A more 'respectable' job. He turns it down. Why would he want it? He knows where he is more comfortable, and that's serving the customers and being the life and soul of the fish shop.

Flash forward again to 2005, where I am kneeling on a footstool and getting tapped on each shoulder with a sword by the Queen, and only wishing my parents could have been around to see it. I think I can safely say that nothing about that particular situation (indeed, nothing about where my journey ended up taking me altogether) was straightforwardly prefigured in these early scenes from Lodge Lane. On the face of it, it was no more likely that I would end up on that footstool than that I would end up in space.

The lesson being: It's not where you come from, it's where you want to go.

How hard it is to break out of that mindset – that feeling that life has plans for you which are going to outweigh your own plans for life. I remember getting a cab back in to London one afternoon in the mid-1970s, after spending some time with some friends in East Grinstead. I was in *No Sex Please* at this point, and I asked the driver to take me to the Strand Theatre.

'Are you going to see the show there?' he said.

'Actually, I'm in it,' I said.

We fell to talking about what I did and about the play, and he seemed quite interested. I told him he should come and see the show. I reckoned he'd enjoy it. And even if he didn't, there wouldn't be much to lose, would there?

'I can leave a couple of tickets on the door for you, if you like,' I said.

'Oh, no,' he said. 'That's ... theatre.'

'Yeah,' I said, 'but really, it's a show for anyone, this one. It's a fun night.' I impressed upon him that it was a bunch of laughs, a farce. He'd get to see me hanging from a picture above a doorframe in a pair of boxer shorts.

I couldn't convince him.

'Nah,' he said. 'It's theatre. That's not for the likes of me.'

Now, maybe he'd read the reviews. Or maybe he'd just remembered that he'd seen me in something else. Or maybe I shouldn't have mentioned the bit about the boxer shorts. But I really don't think so. From the expression on his face and the way he spoke, this person genuinely felt that theatre was, in and of itself, something that excluded him, that it was 'above his station'. Not for the likes of him.

It's a tiny example of the phenomenon, obviously, relating to a tiny aspect of life. But, in a much more general way, it's a frame of mind that gets in the way for so many of us. It's the sense that the life we lead and the things we can get up to are already set in stone for us. When, in fact, if my experience suggests anything, it's that they aren't set in stone at all.

Mind you, on reflection, if that cab driver *had* read the reviews, he would have seen some things. The critical response appeared, of course, three years before this conversation, in 1971, when Michael Crawford was in the starring role, and ... well, blimey. Talk about getting a panning. *No Sex Please* was written by Alistair Foot and Anthony Marriott. Tony Marriott had written scripts for *The Avengers* and for the Gerry Anderson puppet series, *Fireball XL5*, and he had already had a big success with a farce, too – *Uproar in the House*, which ran in the West End for two years. He was an established writer, then. And yet he thought *No Sex Please* was about to end his career. It was absolutely savaged by the critics, ripped to shreds, dismissed as 'the most wit-less play in London' and described, with a shudder, as 'forlorn porn'.

Forlorn porn? Really? I must have missed those bits. It was *about* forlorn porn, in the sense that the plot hinged on an assistant bank manager and his new wife innocently writing away for some Scandinavian glassware and instead receiving through the post a torrent of explicit Swedish books and films, which they then have to conceal to avoid humiliation and scandal. But as for *containing* forlorn porn ... no.

OK, you could point to the fact that it flopped on Broad-way: the US production lasted only sixteen performances before it closed in ignominy. But I guess the clue was in the title: *No Sex Please, We're BRITISH*. The extremely British attitudes to sex that the piece depended on for many of its laughs were probably always going to meet with blank-faced confusion among US audiences.

Nevertheless, in the UK the show had a real impact: 6,761 performances between 1971 and 1987 tell their own story. (I was there for eighteen months of those, before I decided it was time to move on; Ronnie Corbett took over from me.) That title went into the language. People still constantly turn out variations on that 'No – please, we're

DAVID JASON

British' [fill in gap accordingly] theme. Sometimes you have to take the verdict of the audience over the verdict of the critics, and this was a stonewall case of that.

Speaking personally, I'll always be thankful for that show. It was the first time I saw my name in red lights on a West End theatre hoarding – quite the thrill. The stage manager said I should go out and take a photograph of it. Whether he thought that was as high as my career was likely to take me, so I needed to record it and savour the memories, I have no idea. At the time, I would probably have concurred with him. Your name in lights in the West End? How does it get any better than that? I went outside and took the picture.

Also, that feeling of being part of a production that's absolutely flying and making a noise that's being heard way beyond its own little quarter of London is fantastic and, as I know to my cost, extremely rare. And it had audiences literally rolling in the aisles. On a number of separate occasions I was able to look out from the stage and see where someone had actually shaken themselves loose from their seat because they were laughing so much, and were now technically creating a fire hazard on the steps. And that doesn't often happen (although I did once roll into an aisle myself, but we'll come to that in due course).

Following in the footsteps of a masterful slapstick performer like Michael Crawford, and taking what he had done and trying to find some way to make it my own, was the biggest challenge I had faced up to that point. The production also put me on a stage with some really top-rate actors, people way ahead of me in terms of experience who were only ever going to cause me to up my game. Simon Williams and Belinda Carroll I've already mentioned. Then there was the excellent Liza Goddard, who had been in *Take Three Girls* and whose career was on a rapid rise. Liza once described me as 'one of the most marvellous farceurs'. At least, I think she said 'farceurs'.

Also in the cast eventually was Jean Kent – an actual and bona fide film star. I grew up watching her movies. She was in Gainsborough Pictures melodramas, *Fanny by Gaslight* with Stewart Granger, *The Wicked Lady*, *Caravan* and *Trottie True*; she was with Rex Harrison in *The Rake's Progress*, and with John Mills in *Waterloo Road*. Later she was with Michael Redgrave in the film version of Terence Rattigan's *The Browning Version*. When we worked together I discovered she was an actor, not a star. That would be the biggest compliment I could pay anyone in our trade. I was very proud to be asked to write a tribute for her funeral in 2013.

A funny moment occurred when Eamonn Andrews appeared in the Strand Theatre foyer to nab Jean for *This Is Your Life*. That show was always very delicately set up, and what normally happened in the wake of those surprise moments was the 'victim' was put straight in a car and taken to Thames Television Studios before they could get cold feet or wander off somewhere and wreck months of prior planning and a tight shooting schedule. Somehow, though, in the car on this occasion, Jean persuaded Eamonn to make a detour to her flat so that she could change into another dress for the show.

'I'll be literally sixty seconds,' she promised him.

Eamonn, despite the fact that he would have been desperately clock-watching, agreed to this. He accompanied Jean into the lift at her apartment block – and the lift got stuck. I think the pair of them were in there for about ten minutes, hammering on the buttons and the doors, with nobody responding. Eamonn was probably on the verge of a nervous breakdown when the lift suddenly, for no reason at all, unless it was a fan of the show, shuddered back into life and completed the journey.

Undeterred, Eamonn was to stomp on stage with his big red book during another West End production I was involved in, a decade after this – *Look No Hans*. This time he was surprising Richard Vernon. Richard's storied career included the privilege of playing a disapproving businessman trapped in a train carriage with The Beatles in *A Hard Day's Night*. 'Give us a kiss,' says John Lennon. Many people would have felt able to retire on the strength of that claim to fame alone, but Richard had a thousand more. That was the night that Wendy Craig accused Richard of having 'the wickedest twinkle of any actor I ever worked with'.

The lesson being: we should all live to have Wendy Craig sing the praises of our wicked twinkles.

Incidentally, I hear you tentatively enquiring: 'Did Eamonn ever arrive from stage left with a book bearing your name on its cover and then whisk you away to a studio to make the past and all your friends and relatives flash before your startled eyes?'

Well, thank you for asking. And the simple truth is that, no, Eamonn did not. Nor did Michael Aspel, who later took over the show. And thank God for that. I would have run a mile. I would have become only the third person in history to flee the show's embrace. (The first was the author Richard Gordon, who greeted Eamonn with a robust 'Balls!' – but he eventually relented and the show went ahead. The second was the footballer Danny Blanchflower who, according to Eamonn in his autobiography, 'fled like a greyhound from a trap', and wasn't persuaded to come back.) I mean no disrespect to the show, which I used to enjoy watching enormously. And I certainly mean no disrespect to Eamonn and Michael – consummate professionals both. I've enjoyed sitting in the audience a couple of times, too.

But the undivided attention of the room and surprise parties ... I'm afraid that's two of my least favourite things in a sandwich. If Eammon had got stuck in a lift with me on the way to the *This Is Your Life* set, I'm telling you: that lift would have stayed stuck.

There's a very good story about Ronnie Barker in this area. The tale goes that his wife Joy was helping to organise Ronnie's appearance on the show and having all sorts of hush-hush phone conversations – to the point where Ronnie became rather suspicious and began to wonder whether Joy was having an affair. His suspicion only increased when he happened on a piece of paper with the name 'Brian' and a phone number written on it. Ronnie tremblingly rang the number and a voice answered, saying, 'Hello, *This Is Your Life* office.' At which point the show had to be scrapped.

As I say, a good story – but, alas, entirely apocryphal. Although he had helped organise Ronnie Corbett's appearance on the show, Ronnie made Joy swear to tell him if the producers ever came after her about doing the same thing for him. That kind of thing just wasn't what Ronnie B was about. It would have made him intensely uncomfortable, and I shared that attitude with him.

Because, yes, we need to look back in order to understand our lives. But if it's all right with you, I'd rather do it in my own time, and not in front of cameras and a live audience. I'd rather do it here, dear reader, with you.

CHAPTER THREE

On celluloid dreams and the view from the cheap seats

The first glimpses of other worlds and other possibilities: for me, I realise, as I look back, those glimpses came at the cinema. In the tip-up seats at the Odeon in North Finchley, this would have been, and at the Gaumont, where a young and vertically challenged person such as myself could perch himself on the raised seat-edge and thereby get a view around the head of the vertically unchallenged person who unfailingly seemed to park himself directly in front of me. Or at any rate, I could perch up there until my backside grew numb, and then I would have to drop the seat, reluctantly, and sit down properly.

Meanwhile, up on the screen, bigger than any man has a right to be, John Wayne would be looking down directly at me with a Stetson on his head and a gun in his hand, and saying: 'Make one false move and you're dead where you sit.'

Blimey. That was it. The hair was up on the back of my neck and I was riveted to the seat. Or, rather, to the front edge of the seat.

You probably already know this from the swagger in my walk and the celebrated speed with which I pull a six-gun from a holster, but I absolutely idolised John Wayne as a kid. And, in retrospect, my childhood was a very good time to be idolising him, too. Wayne was arguably in his pomp when I started getting taken to the cinema. I was able to see him in *Fort Apache*, *She Wore a Yellow Ribbon*, *Rio Grande* – all those great John Ford Westerns. Not that the name John Ford would have meant very much to me; I learned much later that there were these people called directors who shaped films. At the time all that mattered was that it was a film with John Wayne in it. You would turn up on the strength of John Wayne's name alone. I wasn't looking any further down the credits. I didn't feel I needed to.

I saw him in *Red River* and *The Quiet Man*. Then in 1956, going to the cinema with friends and unaccompanied by adults now, I saw him in *The Searchers* – all of these terrific Westerns, coming at you in a seemingly endless stream, transporting you to the unthinkably vast expanses and strange rocky outcrops of the American West. I saw so many cowboy films in those days that I sometimes felt I knew the nooks and crannies of Monument Valley as well as I knew the shops on Finchley High Road.

Much later, as an adult in 1975, I would see Wayne in *Brannigan*, playing a Chicago detective who has been sent to London to track down a mobster and take him back to the States. I think Richard Attenborough was in that film, too, and Judy Geeson. But it all felt wrong to me. I found my childhood memories hard to leave behind. John Wayne in London? Playing a cop? For me, he never managed to cross the divide from Western hero to modern hero. I didn't even really want to think of him in the army or the navy or the air force as a World War II combatant, although, of course, he had a lot of success in those kinds of roles. If he wasn't on a horse, it was never going to be quite the same for me.

James Stewart once said, with perhaps more than a hint of longing: 'People identify with me, but they dream of being John Wayne.' We certainly did. He was tough, he was noble. He had a charisma that seemed to flood off the screen without any particular effort on his part. And he had that hypnotic voice – which we could all do impressions of, of course. Wayne was a handy subject for a beginner in mimicry because the key characteristic of his voice was its slowness: the voice gave you time to get your mouth around it, in the same way that toffee did.

What I didn't know (and probably would have refused to believe) was that by 1950, John Wayne was wearing a hairpiece under that Stetson. Just like I did, you will recall, albeit not under a Stetson, when I played Granville in *Open*

All Hours. It all thinned out for him up there during the 1940s, apparently. Tell me about it, John. Happens to the very best of us.

The lesson being: you might have more in common with John Wayne than you think.

And then there was Alan Ladd, another great cowboy. I saw Ladd in *Shane* when I was thirteen, and I was transfixed. I was so besotted, in fact, that I eventually wrote away for his autograph. I can't think now where I would have got the idea from. Perhaps a schoolmate suggested it to me; perhaps I saw an advertisement at the back of somebody's *Photoplay* magazine. But I wrote away and, sure enough, in due course, back came a small black and white photo of Ladd with a mass-printed signature across it. Which I suppose, in retrospect, was a disappointing outcome: not the actual autograph from Ladd's own hand, but a print of it – evidence of a publicity machine in action. It didn't seem disappointing to me, though. On the contrary, this was bounty from another planet – and contact with another world. It seemed unfathomable to me that you could write off to Hollywood and get a response of any kind, printed or otherwise. I squirreled that photo away in a little book.

Ladd was not tall: he was only five foot five – even shorter than me. Perhaps that was something that instinctively drew me to him – although obviously it would have had to be instinctive because his height, or lack of it, was very carefully kept from you. All sorts of elaborate measures, I would later learn, had been taken to ensure that he continued to look powerful and dominant, not least in his constant choice of co-star – Veronica Lake (height: four foot ten). Directors were standing Ladd on boxes, standing the people he was talking to in specially dug trenches, you name it – all this trickery, of course, going, literally, over my head in the Gaumont as I stared up at him in awe of his presence. They would lower the height of doorknobs for his scenes and there's apparently at least one famous sequence where they forget to make the adjustment and Ladd ends up opening a door with a handle at nipple height. Very glad I didn't notice. Cherished impressions would have crumbled.

I liked George Raft, too, in gangster films. And I stared in awe at Jimmy Cagney tap dancing in *Yankee Doodle Dandy*, moving from the chest down, with everything above that completely stationary. It was a side of the tough guy that you rarely saw, although, of course, his background was in vaudeville and he had all these skills in his locker.

But nothing beat a Western. Give me Rory Calhoun in *The Yellow Tomahawk* or *Four Guns to the Border*, and I was happy. Calhoun was another early impression of mine: I could do a decent version of his voice, with its slightly sibilant 's'. I only wished I could do a version of his chiselled jaw. Outside the cinema, I would stare in wonder at the posters, pinned up behind glass in the display cases, with their painted pictures of the stars and their tantalising sketched hints of the action that lay in store. You have to imagine the impact of these wonderful pictures against a background of post-war deprivation in north London. Don't get me wrong: we had horses in Finchley, too. But they were normally pulling the window-cleaner's cart, and you wouldn't have fancied that particular nag to get you over a rocky plain in a hurry, nor even up the road all that sharpish, on the evidence of it. The sheer colours of those cinema posters would ring out at you in a way that was quite unlike anything in the generally quite grey and smoggy world that was around you. They conjured something that was instantly exotic, like a display of tropical fruit, which we also never saw.

And that sense of a colour and vibrancy far beyond your everyday life was true, in fact, of everything about the experience of going to the cinema. We would go twice a week for the most part. My mother would take me, with my brother Arthur at first, until I was eleven and he was eighteen and went off to do his National Service. Sometimes my father would come, certainly when I was smaller – a Humphrey Bogart film might tempt him out. But mostly it was Mum, who was prepared to pitch up with me and see pretty much whatever was on. We would typically go in turn to the Odeon and the Gaumont. And then some weeks we would hop on the bus up to the Bohemia at Church End, where the films tended to be slightly more arty and a little less mainstream, not that we were particularly fussed. We just wanted to go to the cinema.

You took your chances wherever you went because you wouldn't always get in. I can still see the sandwich boards they used to put out at the head of the queues – one for the two-and-threes and one for the one-and sixes, which were the cheap seats. That was our queue: one shilling and sixpence for the grown-ups, ninepence for the kids. I can remember being out there in all weathers, stamping in the driven snow on some occasions. The uniformed commissionaire would come out and call down the line: 'Is there a three?' And three people together would be hauled forward to occupy the last remaining seats.

Nobody complained. These days, one suspects, it would be, 'Oi! I've been 'ere two hours, me!' followed by a bit of a scene. But that was the system and nobody seemed to buck it. Out would come the 'HOUSE FULL' sign, meaning you'd have to head off home and try again on Thursday.

It's hard to convey now just how grand those cinemas felt, once you got inside. You were under no illusions about it: you were somewhere special – a veritable palace of pleasure and hospitality. Cinemas were modern. They were clean. They were well lit by electricity. They had a nice smell to them. They had amazing curtains. They even had indoor lavatories, if you can believe it.

And here was the biggest treat of all: they were warm. Properly warm. Warm throughout. Not for the cinema two struggling grates that toasted your front but not your back. Cinemas offered 360-degree warmth.

Bundle together those attractions – the aroma, the cleanliness, the princely indoor facilities, the flattering grandness of it all and the heat – and you can see why the White family and our peers might have hurried to the Gaumont, or the Odeon, or the Bohemia in a state of eager anticipation, whatever was on the bill. One can argue long and hard about the reasons why cinema has ceased to exert the magnetic power over audiences that it enjoyed in the late forties and fifties. But one should never leave out of one's calculations the simple fact that, by and large, people's homes got nicer.

My mum would happily watch a Western, but she preferred a romantic film. She wanted to see Rock Hudson and Doris Day. Romance didn't really do it for me the way the cavalry touting rifles did, but it was still good value, and definitely another window onto an altogether unrecognisable world. And I don't just mean the romance although, obviously, that in itself was a source of lasting wonder and something to give a budding youth pause for thought. I'm referring more to the incidental domestic moments. For example, you would see an American fridge, impossibly big, from which someone would casually withdraw a cooked chicken leg and begin to chew on it.

I mean, what? How? In what kind of astonishingly liberated and enriched place was that sort of behaviour possible? And could I go there?

Only in my dreams, at this point. And, of course, also in the cinema.

Our diet was substantially American, but British films began to arrive, too. The first of those that I recall watching was *The Cruel Sea* – Jack Hawkins, Denholm Elliott and Donald Sinden getting menaced by German U-boats and gamely re-fighting the Battle of the Atlantic on behalf of the rest of us. I was glad that they had gone to the trouble, of course, but it simply couldn't seem glamorous to my childish mind in the way the American films seemed glamorous. Nobody ignited the screen quite like the American stars, who made it look so effortless. John Wayne, Jimmy Stewart, Rock Hudson – these actors only needed to be themselves, it seemed, or, at least, that particular version of themselves that they had alighted on for the purposes of making films.

It was the polar opposite of my approach to acting, when I eventually developed one. Be myself? How was that going to work? I wanted to leave myself behind, if I possibly could. My approach was always to be someone else, find another character to disappear into for a while – someone worth watching. Now, there's a theory that this is the fundamental insecurity at the heart of acting: that you are not entirely sure how much you amount to yourself, so you go looking to play the parts of people who amount to more. I'll leave that little thought with you. I can only say that in my case, in due course, the opportunity to be something different seemed to be the greatest and most wonderful gift that acting could bestow on a person. When the world always seemed to be consigning you to your allotted place, acting was there to give you a nudge and remind you that you could escape to somewhere else entirely if you wanted. All of which being said, there's an art to being yourself on a screen, too, and I wallowed in the work of those stars of the forties and fifties – envied them their self-certainty, in fact.

At the cinema, I found out what made an ideal hero, and I found out what made an ideal fridge, and I found out what was funny, too. And what was funny (and my mum seemed to agree) was Jacques Tati in M. *Hulot's Holiday*. I cannot over-stress the impact made on me, at the impressionable age of thirteen, by going to see that film. I already knew I loved slapstick. What kid doesn't? And I was already a fan of Laurel and Hardy. Who could be anything else? But this thing with Jacques Tati – this was something different again, something on another level.

M. *Hulot's Holiday* was mostly wordless – a throwback in many ways to the silent era, and yet, at the same time, absolutely dependent for comic effect on the possibilities of noise. At heart, though, it was a compilation of sight gags – brilliantly, exquisitely choreographed sight gags, set-ups that appeared to have been whole years in the planning and were now being executed, in a seamless flow, in front of your astonished and mostly tear-filled eyes.

There were gags with suitcases, gags with tennis rackets, gags with pots of paint, gags with dogs and cars and trains and deck chairs and animal-skin rugs and newspapers in the wind … And all of it performed in this wonderfully warm, benign, all-inclusive style without a hint of cruelty or humiliation or a sense that this comedy was created out of anything other than sheer fondness for people and all their eccentricity, and also for things and all their eccentricity. It was like nothing I had ever seen.

And that, dear reader, was the night I ended up literally rolling in the aisles. I no longer recall which of the gags produced the laugh that put me there. Quite likely it was the now legendary moment where Tati's M. Hulot is swallowed by his own paddling boat, which, on a perfectly flat sea, splits and neatly closes around him like the jaws of the least intimidating shark you have ever come across. (You've probably seen this, and if you haven't, you really should.) But there were a hundred other moments in that single film equally capable of eliciting a physical reaction this strong from the thirteen-year-old kid at the end of Row M. And whether I was on the edge of the seat and I over-balanced, or exactly what happened, I no longer recall for sure. But what I can tell you is that I genuinely ended up on the carpet, rendered prostrate by the force of sheer laughter alone.

There are moments in one's life, clearly, where lightbulbs go on in one's brain and stay brightly lit for a very long time, and this, for me, was one of them. I saw that film, and suddenly I had questions: how do you do those things? And, more importantly, how do you *get* to do those things? How does doing those things become a living for you? And what would it be like to be able to fall over in such a way as to make people absolutely lose it?

I think it's no exaggeration to suggest that the quest that would eventually lead me to a certain bar-flap in a certain bistro in Peckham began right there, gasping for breath in front of Jacques Tati at the North Finchley Odeon – or, if not right there, then walking home afterwards in a state of dizzied wonder.

The lesson being: let inspiration take you where it will, including flat on the floor.

I can offer you only one other moment from this period of my life which had anything like an equal impact in terms of inspiration. That was going to watch a recording of *The Goon Show*. I talked about this in my first book, so I won't dwell on it for too long here. But it was a truly formative thing for me, so I need to mention it in this context at least briefly.

We listened to The Goons on the radio at home. I thought they were the greatest thing the radio had to offer – even greater than *Dick Barton: Special Agent*, which was saying something. It wasn't just that they were funny; they were funny in ways that nobody else was funny or had ever seemed to have been funny before. The show came at you fast, too: they worked at an altogether different pace from the shows you were used to listening to. The sound you heard every week was the noise of all existing comedy barriers being broken through and riotously trodden underfoot. The Goons were a law unto themselves and they created a brand of shining idiocy which, again, was all the brighter for being in such contrast to the general backdrop against which we listened to them.

I wrote away for tickets to see the show being taped. The BBC continuity announcer was always letting you know that this was a possibility. You didn't even have to pay. You just had to send off and ask. And, again, as my father always said, 'What costs ya nuffink ... '

So I did, and me and my mate Micky Weedon ended up one weekday night in the Camden Town Theatre, watching the show happen.

In some ways, I suppose, to attend a recording of *The Goon Show* and to see what actually went on in the making of this madness was to risk letting light in on the magic. Maybe it would have been more prudent to allow Eccles, Bluebottle, Bloodnok, Little Jim, Hercules Grytpype-Thynne and all the other bonkers characters that swam out of the radio in a soup of absurd sound effects every week to continue to exist in one's imagination where they could properly flourish. To see those crazy voices emerging from the mouths of some blokes in cardigans while someone else pushed the buttons on the tape machine that had the sound effects on it, and while a floor manager urged you to applaud at the right moment ... well, it could have been a bit of a let-down, all in all.

Yet what I clearly had – just as with writing away for Alan Ladd's autograph – was this urge to reach out towards these unreachable people. And it didn't turn out to be a let-down at all. I must have been in my mid-to-late teens by then, so this was some time after the departure of Michael Bentine in 1952, when The Goons had settled down to become a team of three: Spike Milligan, Peter Sellers and Harry Secombe. Yet even then their identities were largely a mystery to us. Radio performers really did exist behind a thick black curtain of obscurity back then. Secombe was a star beyond the confines of this show, and Milligan I had, I am pretty sure, seen pictures of, but Sellers I had never set eyes on before this night.

Incidentally, the tale of Secombe's first meeting with Milligan is surely one of the great 'first encounter' legends of comedy history. According to Secombe's version of it, they came across each other while on active duty in the war, shortly after Milligan's artillery unit had somehow managed to allow a large and cumbersome howitzer gun to run away down a hill, narrowly missing Secombe, who was sitting further down the slope in another unit's wireless truck. Milligan then allegedly stuck his head through the canvas flap of Secombe's truck and said: 'Has anybody seen a gun?'

To which Secombe replied: 'What colour?'

And the rest was radio history.

Anyway, there they both were, all those years later, on the stage of the Camden Theatre. And there was Sellers, too, making what I thought was an extremely cool entrance, after the other two had appeared, and just in time to speak his first line. They might have been making a radio show, but there was no question that they were just going to stand there around the microphone with their scripts. This was going to be a full-blown theatrical performance. You understood that right from the moment Harry Secombe walked out and plonked down a sign saying *The Goon Show* – plonking it down the wrong way up, of course.

Now, I know how it works, with radio comedy. The deal is, you get the audience warmed up and that warmth comes back to you and into the recording in the form of their laughter. It's no different from filming television in front of a live audience in that sense. But that night at the Goons it seemed to be about so much more than merely getting the audience onside. It was about those three comedians and their natural instinct to perform. They couldn't help themselves.

The other abiding memory from that night is not just of how much pleasure the audience was getting from being in the same room as the Goons, but also of how much pleasure the Goons themselves seemed to be getting from being in the same room as the Goons. The sight of those three, trying to suppress their laughter at each other's gags and at their own and almost continuously on the edge of corpsing, was the most infectiously funny thing I had ever been in a room to witness. Alcohol was forbidden on BBC premises during the rehearsing and recording of shows, and I've since read that the Goons used to get around that by slopping a bit of brandy into milk bottles and smuggling it backstage. So maybe there was some of that going on as well. Let us not probe too deeply, for fear, once again, of letting light in on the magic.

All I will say is that this whole experience spoke very loudly to something deep inside me – almost as loudly as the experience of watching Jacques Tati those few years before it: the madness of it, the slickness of it, the sheer fun of it. Again, I found myself leaving in a state of longing. How great would it be to be a part of something like that? To be part of a tight team that was making people laugh and making itself laugh at the same time? How fantastic would it be if that could turn out to be the central theme of your working life?

Here's another thing I suspect I thought: fat chance.

CHAPTER FOUR

On surviving the lockdown and encountering ghosts of various kinds

'You're not interested, Rodney, are yer? So it's purely epidemic innit, eh?' Derek Trotter

In years to come, small children, their eager eyes alive with curiosity, will ask their grandparents: 'What did you do during the Great Lockdown of 2020, Grandpa?'

And those grandparents will look down at those small children and, employing the gentle but wise tone of those who have lived long and witnessed extraordinary things, say: 'I stayed at home, of course. What do you think I did?'

It was late in March when the UK government eventually decided that the coronavirus wasn't going to go away on its own, and word thereafter came down from on high that practically the entire country was going to have to pull the shutters down and sit this one out for a bit.

Now, I appreciate that there's no good moment to have a global pandemic featuring a frightening virus that science is still in the early days of trying to comprehend and whose destructive effects threaten to overwhelm your country's national health service and crash the economy – but this was especially poor timing, I must say. Having recently set off at a sprint into my ninth decade, I was raring to go and all ready to embark on a busy roster of work which would cement beyond doubt my official position as 'the fourth hardest-working actor in Britain'. (We'll get into the details of that deeply important accolade in a minute.) And what can I tell you? The lockdown well and truly put the kibosh on that particular scheme.

> The lesson being: as hard as it may be to comprehend this, significant world events are no respecters of an actor's diary.

Still, as always, look on the bright side. Had lockdown come just a handful of weeks earlier, bringing its tight restrictions on gatherings and its ban on all but essential travel, it would have nixed my eightieth birthday celebrations, and that would obviously have been an absolute *disaster*.

We kept it simple, in any case. I think you have to. There were a number of ideas for themed parties that I was toying with for a while. At one point, for example, I was going to get the event catered by the people who did Kate Moss's fortieth, which, as I'm sure you will recall, was a splendid four-day affair in the Cotswolds on a Glastonbury Festival theme – live music, face painting, tarot card readers, fire jugglers and so forth.

But then I thought: scratch that. The Cotswolds are cold as all get out in February. Let's go where the sun shines. So instead I simply got hold of a private plane and flew 175 of my closest friends to a little private island I know off Grenada in the Caribbean where we enjoyed five lovely days of parties, limbo dancing on the beautiful white-sand beaches and jet skiing in the warm ocean.

A modest event, then, yes – but no less enjoyable for that. And I don't think I would be speaking out of turn if I suggested that everyone came home with some very precious memories. The performances by Lionel Richie and Stevie Wonder on nights three and four, respectively, seemed to go over well. Sly Stallone and his lovely wife Jennifer had a really good time, I know, and Kim Kardashian told me that she had never been to a party like it, which obviously meant a lot, coming from her. And when Carol Vorderman burst out of that enormous cake on the final night, well ...

OK, not really. I think you know me well enough by now, dear reader, to appreciate that it's not quite in my nature, the partying lark. See my earlier remarks on the pleasures or otherwise of *This Is Your Life*. I had a surprise party thrown for me in my own home on my fiftieth birthday, and it took me the best part of the next thirty years to recover.

Lord, the military levels of planning that had gone into that night, too. I was driving back from Ronnie Barker's in Oxfordshire that afternoon.

'Follow me,' Ronnie had said. 'I can show you a really good route – the back way.'

Really good route, indeed. It was all about delaying my arrival until the appropriate moment, wasn't it? I spent ages that evening being literally driven round the houses by Ronnie Barker. Then, just when I was looking forward to getting into the sitting room and putting my feet up ... Surprise! Friends and relatives poured out of every cupboard, nook and cranny.

No, it was lovely, of course. Wonderful to see them all, and very touching that everyone bothered, and it made my fiftieth very special indeed.

It's just something I never want to go through again if I can avoid it, that's all.

So I think it was fairly clear that my eightieth was never going to see me hankering after a big night on the dance-floor at Annabel's with a confetti cannon and a balloon-drop at midnight. Instead, I celebrated it in a calm and measured manner, and exactly as I would have wished: with my two favourite people – my wife and my daughter – having Sunday lunch at my favourite restaurant.

And a very nice meal we had, too. Cost me an arm and a leg, but an arm and a leg wouldn't have been anywhere near as tasty. And no, I'm not going to tell you where this restaurant is, because then I'll never get a table and it's hard enough already.

Of course, the three of us didn't realise at the time that this birthday treat was going to be just about the last meal out anywhere for a few months. Covid-19 was even then getting its terrifying act together. And, as officially the 'fourth hardest-working actor in the UK', I was about to find myself confronting something of a roadblock.

This 'fourth hardest-working actor' business: I know what you're thinking. Who could possibly be ahead of me on that list? Who else, at this stage in the game, has the dynamism and the flexibility to outwork me at the showbusiness coalface?

Well, I'm in a position to tell you. I am officially the fourth hardest-working actor in the UK after David Tennant, Olivia Colman and Martin Clunes, in that order. Esteemed company indeed.

How do I know this? Because it said so in November 2019 in the results of a survey commissioned by BritBox, the BBC and ITV's streaming service, the results from which were reproduced in the *Radio Times* and the *Daily Mail*, so it must be true.

Just behind me in the list were, in descending order of hard-workingness, Sir Derek Jacobi and Dame Judi Dench, followed by James Nesbitt, Steve Coogan and Sean Bean. To all of whom I suppose my message must be: close, but no cigar, chaps. Well done on making it to that level just below my mighty industrious pinnacle. But maybe work a little harder next time, yes?

I also ranked second in this same survey for 'star power', after Sean Bean. I'm not sure what that means, but I'll take it. And, again, to my illustrious peers lower down the list – Sir Derek again, and Dame Judi – I would merely want to say better luck with the power next time. And if this keeps happening, you might want to look into changing your energy supplier. It's so easy these days. You can do it online in a matter of moments.

Anyway, as the fourth hardest-working actor in the UK, after David Tennant, Olivia Colman and Martin Clunes, I was bound to find lockdown problematic. 'Work from home where possible,' the government was saying. Not possible in my case. Work not possible anywhere, in fact. All film and television productions were brought to an immediate halt. Everything in that line was either cancelled or put on indefinite hold. I was looking at an actor's worst nightmare: an empty schedule. I was the fourth hardest-working actor in the UK with no work.

So how did I get on, as March turned into April and April teetered on towards May, and then as May in turn teetered on towards June? Not especially well, I have to say. Permit me to demonstrate exactly how it went by reproducing here a few of the earliest entries from my 2020 Lockdown Diary.

Thursday 26 March

Lockdown, day two. Go for a walk on my own, in compliance with government recommendations vis-à-vis an hour of exercise. See a lone figure coming towards me on a single track path. This is possibly a first encounter for both of us under the new lockdown rules of engagement. Both of us seem very keen to do our duty, as regards social distancing. When we are within about ten feet of each other, I plunge backwards into the bush on the left and he plunges backwards into the bush on the right. We then sidle gingerly past each other, dragging our rears across the hedgerow. Once clear of each other's threat, we drag ourselves out, rejoin the path and continue. Spend the rest of the walk home removing thorns from my posterior.

Friday 27 March

Lockdown, day three. Go to the supermarket with Gill. There is a long, responsibly distanced queue. People are being extremely patient and also extremely thoughtful. Less advantaged shoppers are constantly being allowed to go forwards to the front of the queue. After an hour, Gill and I are forty feet further away from the entrance than we were when we arrived. We give up and go home.

Saturday 28 March

Lockdown, day four. Quite bored. In the afternoon decide to pass some time by looking out of the window from my chair and counting the number of people who walk past in the lane. It's not a busy lane. Get to two and fall asleep.

Sunday 29 March

Lockdown, day five. Even more bored. Decide to use the time to paint the spare room. Open a tin of paint that has been knocking about for some time. Look inside the tin. Look around the room. Decide to go downstairs and stare out of the window instead.

Monday 30 March

Lockdown, day six. Gill puts head round door. Says, 'I'm just going to scalp my mother.' Then leaves. Ponder this after she has gone. Sounds like something to do, I guess – and heaven knows, we need a project. But how is she going to manage it? Her mother is miles away, in Yorkshire. Eventually, curious, go out to kitchen. Find Gill in a face-to-face conversation with her mother using her mobile phone. Skype, then, not scalp. Will have to get used to this distinction. Seems like there will be a lot of scalping going on during lockdown. I mean, Skypeing.

Tuesday 31 March

Lockdown, day seven. Still bored.

Wednesday 1 April

April Fool! Also: I'm bored. Also: lockdown, day ... losing count now.

And so it went on, one largely featureless day blending seamlessly into the next, the very days of the week ceasing to have any real distinction between them. And it struck me eventually, in a way that cast, I don't mind saying, a cold and clammy hand around my kidneys: this must be what retirement is like.

If you're lucky enough to do something you love, retirement is not something you long for. Indeed, it's something you hope to avoid, if you possibly can, although, in my case, given what I do for a living, you are aware that your powers are ultimately going to be limited in this regard. The entertainment business, whether you like it or not, rather takes the matter of retirement out of your hands. In acting, it's not you that retires from the business, it's the business that retires from you. It walks away when it has had enough of you and finds someone else to play with. In the meantime, if working is the thing that gets you up and going, you inevitably worry a bit about what it would feel like if the work wasn't there any more. In lockdown, in common with every other actor in the country, I got a vision of that. And I was absolutely sure I didn't like it.

When I first went along to present myself to the agent Richard Stone at the Richard Stone Partnership, Richard asked me, 'What do you most want to achieve?' And I replied, 'I want to work.' I didn't say I had a deep yearning to be famous, because that wouldn't have been true. I didn't say I wanted to be able to pull down as much bunce as I possibly could in order to be driving around in an E-Type Jag by the end of the month because, although that was undoubtedly a nice idea, I genuinely couldn't have claimed it was the primary motivation here. (I also knew enough about the business to understand that it wasn't straightforwardly in an agent's gift to make that happen for a young and mostly unknown actor, as I was at that stage.) What I wanted, very simply, was to work – to BE an actor.

And, with Richard's help, work I did – moving from one thing to the next because that seemed to me to be the fun of it and also the privilege of it and actually even the whole point of it.

I was eventually entrusted, within the Richard Stone Partnership, to the endlessly patient Meg Poole, who still represents me fifty years later. Which is quite a miracle, really, because I'm afraid, back at the beginning, I was one of those tiresome actors who, on any day without work in it, would be dreaming up excuses to call their agent.

'Yeah, hi! ... Yeah, I know, third time today! ... But yeah, what it is; I was just thinking, I haven't heard from [actor inserts name of random colleague here] in a while. Do you know what he's up to? Oh, and ... anything for me?'

Basically, I brought to being a self-employed actor the same attitude that I had brought to being a self-employed electrician. 'Got a job that needs doing in my line? Yeah, I can do that.' I guess I didn't really know any other way to think about it. Voice-overs, small parts in touring productions, supporting roles in summer seasons – I took 'em all.

And commercials? Absolutely. Why not? I have sat in a giant teacup and been pelted with enormous polystyrene sugar lumps in order to demonstrate the flow-through virtues of a well-known brand of teabag. I have responsibly informed the nation: 'There's around 300 crispy bits in every Toffee Crisp.' (They didn't ask me to count them, fortunately.) I've stood up tall for a leading building society against the kinds of bank that make people pay to use their current account. ('The Light Brigade made less ridiculous charges.') I could go on. There have been countless other pieces of work like this, which in some ways are probably best left to float down history's winding stream and disappear off to the hazy horizon.

And do you know what? I don't regret a single one of them.

Not one. Not even the business in the teacup, where it turned out that polystyrene sugar lumps carry more of a clout than you might think. And this is not about some fancy notion of 'paying my dues' or 'putting in the hard yards', because that wasn't how I thought of it. I don't regret any of them because all of them were better than sitting at home twiddling my thumbs and wondering whether Hollywood was going to call.

From my point of view, as long as I was out there somewhere I was practising the trade, and for as long as I was practising the trade I was learning the trade, too. I would recommend that approach to any actor who is starting out – and maybe there is a little grain of truth at the heart of it which extends beyond acting, in fact, and into all types of work. Don't pass up the opportunity to get valuable experience under your belt because you're waiting for some notional 'bigger call' further down the line.

Grab the little bits of work as they present themselves and squeeze them for whatever they can offer you. Because nothing is ever really wasted if you take the right attitude towards it. You're salting away a little bit of knowledge every time you do something that works – and you're possibly salting away even more knowledge every time you do something that doesn't work. Take this from the fourth most hard-working actor in television according to a poll in 2019. All of those tiny pieces of experience add up.

And who knows? One of those seemingly humdrum jobs might just turn out to be the opportunity that leads to your major break. It certainly was in my case, as we shall see.

The lesson being: put yourself out there.

Not much putting yourself out there during a pandemic, though. Not much putting yourself anywhere, I found, apart from into your armchair at home. A person's mind can start to turn unhelpfully inward on itself in such circumstances, there's no question. In my case, things came to such a pass that I started seeing ghosts.

And not just any old ghosts: the ghost of the former lady of this house, whose restless spirit was long said to roam the property, as I was informed at the time of purchase, but who had hitherto lain dormant through all the years of my occupancy, only choosing to reveal herself now.

Picture your author, if you will, at work one afternoon at the table in his kitchen-cum-dining room – at work on this very tome, indeed. The house is otherwise empty of people, his wife and daughter being elsewhere, in dutiful compliance, of course, with government regulations on either exercise or shopping for essentials. As the ideas pour forth in a torrent from the writer's fevered brain, the sole sound that breaks the silence is the frantic scratching of quill on parchment. (I really must get round to getting a typewriter one day – and soon, before they go out of fashion and get replaced by whatever people will think of next, which you can be sure they will, progress being the inexorable force that it is.)

On the author labours, his head lowered, his eyes and his concentration wholly absorbed by the words that are unfurling across the page in fresh ink, until, just narrowly above the frame of the glasses on his nose, he becomes dimly aware of a movement – a very slight movement, but a movement nonetheless.

The top of the empty chair at the opposite end of the table has just shifted.

I stop writing and stare hard at the chair, waiting for it to move again. It doesn't do so, though, so I conclude that I must have imagined it. I shake my head, adjust my glasses and return to my labours.

More words pour forth. But wait: there it is again, in my peripheral vision. A small but distinct shuffling of the chair at the far end of the table, a movement which is over almost as soon as it begins. Once more I stop, and once more I stare.

And this time, as I watch, the chair moves again.

By now the hairs, such as they are, are creeping up on the back of my neck and it is as if an ice-cold fingertip has begun to travel the length of my spine. Shifting chairs? Unexplained movements in an empty house? I would be feeling less spooked if a conversation I once had with the previous owner of this property wasn't now repeating itself in my mind.

'Any hauntings?' I had jovially asked, as I was looking around the place, with my heart already set on buying it.

'Just the one,' said the seller, equally jovially. 'A woman who lived here sometime in the 1800s, who died in mysterious circumstances and who is alleged to pop back and check over her old abode every now and again. Never seen her myself, though.'

'Well, as long as the rent keeps arriving,' I quipped.

Oh, how we laughed.

Yet even as I am recalling this, the chair again begins to move, much more vigorously now, almost as if taunting me for my original disbelief, and there is simultaneously a noise of scuffling, somewhere below the chair, at that end of the table.

By this point, I am rigid with what I can only describe, dear readers, as fright. True, the old girl with the dodgy past has shown no inclination to reveal herself at any point in the many intervening years since we moved in. We have lived a happy and notably unbothered life here to this point – a life entirely without poltergeists or anything that Yvette Fielding and the *Most Haunted* team would be particularly interested in making a programme about.

But maybe that old girl from the nineteenth century has merely been biding her time. Maybe all she needed was a global pandemic and a nationwide lockdown. Maybe her time is now.

Very slowly, and truly rattled by the thought of what I might be about to see, I bend myself sideways and downwards to look under the table.

I have no idea when Tuffy, our large and lazy Labrador, left her bed and crept in here for company. I only know it would have been decent of her to give me some notice. I also know that lockdown has brought me to my lowest point so far: genuinely interpreting the movements of my own dog as evidence of paranormal activity.

A low point, then, but also, as low points can be, the inspiration I possibly needed to get a grip and turn this lockdown situation around. Enough climbing the walls, and enough retirement. The country may have been closed for actorly business, but other people seemed to be finding a way. Others weren't wallowing in their under-employment and misinterpreting Labradors as spirits. Instinctively resourceful types were getting off their backsides and finding creative outlets for their talents even within these strictly confined and unhelpful circumstances. Home-made videos of performances and diversions of all kinds were springing up all over Twitter and Instagram and Tik Tok and all sorts of other media outlets which, I confess, I don't have the strongest handle on, but for the existence of which I am happy to take the word of my daughter.

It was obvious, as I looked around me and digested the situation, that people were stepping up and doing their bit. The theatres might have been dark and the film sets abandoned, but the entertainment community was coming together. Comics of all stripes were doing at-home routines, or posting skits and impressions. Sports commentators, with no sport to commentate on, were at home recording commentaries on the scenes outside their windows, just for laughs. The BBC golf commentator Andrew Cotter was commentating on the activities of his dogs – to great and deserved acclaim. Gary Barlow was sitting in his home studio singing down-the-line duets with other pop stars who were also stranded at home. Even sensationally brave NHS staff on the frontline were picking themselves up off the floor in their breaks to perform morale-lifting dance routines.

Clearly it was beholden upon entertainers such as myself – a knight of the realm, indeed – to do what they could for their country in a period of difficulty, as entertainers have always done in times of trouble down the years. I realised that I had been spending my energy forlornly staring out of the window and mistaking my dog for a ghost, when in fact I needed to be tapping into my inner Dame Vera Lynn – and never more urgently than when the great Dame herself finally headed off in June for a well-earned rest at the magnificent and inspiring age of 103.

Inevitably, then, the question was in my mind: what useful service could I possibly render my nation in this time of need? What succour was I best placed and most suited to provide? A rendition of 'The White Cliffs of Dover'? Perhaps as a duet with Gary Barlow? Possibly not a good idea. Ask anyone who has ever heard me sing. Fact: when I sing, piano lids within a hundred-yard radius automatically close. I once, as a young actor, was asked to sing at an audition. I immediately regretted it. The people holding the audition regretted it even more. In fact, I have a feeling the show closed then and there.

So, no singing. But what though? What could I bring to the table that would uplift the country at this hour?

I racked my brains. One thought that occurred to me was that maybe I could lead the nation in an online morning PE class. That would be a valuable service, surely, in a time when schools were closed and parents were at home trying to occupy their children and keep them active. Unfortunately, before I could even get up the ladder to fetch my old plimsolls out of the attic, someone called Joe Wicks had nipped in to assume that role. He seemed to have it fairly well covered, too, so I decided to drop back and let him get on with it. I was too late. I should have moved quicker.

What about home baking, then? Home baking seemed to be enjoying a bit of a vogue in this crisis. Was there anything practical that I could provide the country with in that line? A home cooking course, sharing my tips and tricks for perfect cakes and pastries, perhaps? Maybe I could call it *David Jason's Buns of Steel*.

Actually, that title would have worked for a fitness class as well as a cookery class. Possibly a combination of the two, then? Squats and dough-kneading in one highly serviceable lockdown package?

Again, though, somehow that idea seemed to falter at the development stage.

And then I had an idea: Trigger's Broom. It was the perfect moment for it, surely.

You will recall, most likely, Trigger from *Only Fools* and his medal-winning road-sweeping tool, which, to the great approval of the local council, was still going strong after twenty years – perhaps in no small measure due to the fact that it had had seventeen new heads and fourteen new handles in that time. In a great example of the sensational range of John Sullivan's writing, Trigger's proud account of how he came by a medal from the council enabled that episode to raise the great and as yet unresolved philosophical question: "Ow the 'ell can it be the same bloody broom, then?'

(Scholars of classical antiquity, such as myself, will recognise this as a version of Plutarch's Ship of Theseus paradox. Scholars of pop music history – also myself – will equally well recognise it as another way of expressing the famous Sugababes paradox: to wit, was it still correct to call them the Sugababes once all the original members of that poptastic all-girl combo had been replaced? I often lie awake at night, pondering that mystery.)

However, it wasn't the longevity of Trigger's broom I was interested in at this point in the pandemic; it was the length of it, something less open to philosophical debate. Although, I suppose, if we're going to be pedantic about it, 'how long is a broom?' is another of those open-ended questions. But let's not go there. In the early days of the pandemic, people had to become used to the idea of maintaining a two-metre distance from one another in public spaces – not easy to do without a visual gauge of reference. And that's where I was going to come in.

Imagine yourself holding Trigger's broom in an outstretched arm: that's two metres, right there, or as close to it as makes no difference. With 'Trigger's broom' firmly established as the nationally endorsed unit of measurement for effective social distancing, people would also have an accessible and non-aggressive verbal tool with which to police the behaviour of others, vis-à-vis their personal space. Should anyone encroach upon your personal exclusion zone, you would be in a position to issue the friendly warning, 'Trigger's', or simply 'broom', and allow them to adjust their distance.

I even devised a slogan – 'Trigger's broom: we'll beat this soon' – which was at least as comprehensible as any of the government's jingles in this area, some of which we'll have cause to discuss shortly.

It all seemed to make a lot of sense. With my wife and daughter in the important production roles, I recorded a short video clip in the garden, explaining the Trigger's broom social distancing method. The internet, like a magic pigeon, then took the resulting message to the world, and the rest, as you will be aware, is lockdown history. Social distancing was impeccably observed from that moment on, even by government advisers, the virus was controlled and the NHS saved, and the country moved forward as one into a new era of health and prosperity.

Or something like that. I know the idea went over well with the *Only Fools and Horses* Appreciation Society, at any rate.

Don't thank me: any other entertainer in my position would have done the same. I, meanwhile, could take the quiet satisfaction, at the beginning of my eighty-first year, of having taken my first steps along the road to becoming what I believe we now refer to as 'an influencer'. Shortly after this, my attention was drawn to an article on the BBC News website offering guidance on social distancing and using, would you believe, an outheld broom as a unit of measurement.

But was I given any credit in the article for this mathematical breakthrough – Triggernometry, as mathematicians around the globe now refer to it? Sadly not. Ah, well. Sometimes one must be content to be a prophet without honour in one's own land, like what the Bible said.

The lesson being: it's the message that's important, not the messenger.

Trigger's broom was not my only virtual triumph during the lockdown period, although, I will concede, my involvement in the second one was a little more tangential. At one point the BBC delved into its archive and put up on its website pictures of empty sets from various comedy shows down the years.

A number of those sets were more than familiar to me. There in all its glory was Arkwright's shop from the first series of *Open All Hours* in the mid-1970s, with the magazines hanging up above the counter and the outsized weighing scales and a sign promoting 'Carnation Pilchards' at 35p and the wonderful chaos that could bring gardening tools, plastic laundry baskets and boxes of Quaker Harvest Crunch together in the same tiny emporium.

Then there were a couple of sets from *Porridge* from the same era: the prison landing and the rudimentary, wood-furnished prison cell where Ronnie Barker's Fletcher and Richard Beckinsale's Godber once reclined, and where I occasionally joined them (once again old before my time) as Blanco.

And then there were four sets from *Only Fools and Horses*. There was the Trotters' Peckham flat from circa 1982 – the magnificent brown and orange curtains, the busy wallpaper, and, suffocating the battered old armchairs, the usual clutter, including a stack of traffic cones, a surprising number of mops and a preponderance of crates of Spanish oranges – 'so fresh they were playing castanets this morning,' no doubt.

There were two interiors of the Nag's Head, with its tiled floor, its dark red and brown colour scheme and that stupid stuffed white rabbit in a glass box above the bar. (Did anybody ever explain the provenance of that white rabbit?) And then there was the wine bar set from 1988, from the 'Yuppy Love' episode, where Del and Trigger attempt to play it cool and where the bar had a flap that would come in very handy for a certain piece of comic business that you possibly remember. (Obviously the Nag's Head had a bar-flap that could have been used for the same purpose at almost any point in the show's history. But when you think about it, it wouldn't have been the same. Del needed to be on unfamiliar territory for this gag to work in its full glory, and John, who had seen something like this actually happen to some unsuspecting bloke in a pub in Balham, saved it up for just the right moment.)

While we're on that subject, can I just say that I've always been delighted to see that little moment from 'Yuppy Love' come out top in 'Greatest TV Moment' polls, which it still seems to do on a startlingly regular basis. At the same time, I must confess to feeling a little bit uncomfortable about that 1999 poll on Channel Four, when the TV moments it came out on top of included film of the assassination of John F. Kennedy and the coverage of Winston Churchill's funeral.

I mean, I'm not trying to spoil anybody's fun here, and I'll happily take the accolade: but that's comparing apples with pears just a touch, isn't it? I mean, there's comedy history and then there's ... well, your actual *history*. But no matter. Let me at least insist that nobody was hurt in the making of that bar-flap stunt. Well, except for me, of course. (Some light bruising to the arms and shoulder, but the crash mat out of sight on the other side of the bar took the worst of it.)

Anyway, that bistro, with its classy neon cocktail signs and all, was there among this collection of set pictures, along with others from shows like *Hancock's Half Hour*, *Steptoe and Son*, *Dad's Army*, *Yes, Prime Minister* and *Fawlty Towers*. And I have to say I found those images stirred some powerful emotions for me. Obviously they brought back memories of some truly great days – shots of the old workplace. At the same time, there was something about the sets being empty that felt emotional, too – not teeming with life and noise and buzz, as I remember them. Very much places from the past.

And yet these places from the past seemed to have a role in the present, too. The reason for this burst of nostalgia on the BBC's part? Well, the pictures formed a little gimmick that went under the title 'The Joy of Sets'. I wonder how many members of the younger generation instantly picked up the punning allusion there to the famous seventies sex manual, with its educational drawings of a man (normally bearded) and a woman (normally not bearded) combining imaginatively, and often extremely impressively, in the pursuit of fleshly pleasures. Many was the bookshop which, in the heyday of that great work, chose to display *The Joy of Sex* in the fiction section.

No matter. The BBC's instructions, as supplied on the website, for the use and enjoyment of 'The Joy of Sets' were as follows – and here I can do no better than quote them in full, for reasons that will become apparent:

'Click on an image to bring up a full quality downloadable version, right click and select "Save image as ... ", then set it as your background image in your video conferencing application.'

Now, by my calculation, only about three words in that entire paragraph would have been comprehensible at the time when any of the sets that I have mentioned were built.

Between you and me, only about three words of that paragraph are comprehensible to me even now, actually. A video conferencing application? Well, I'm guessing it's got something in common with the means by which my wife was able to scalp my mother-in-law, but I'm mostly shooting in the dark here and I don't mind admitting it.

Still, it gave me pause, I can tell you. Here those sets were, getting on for forty years later and more, being offered up as fun backgrounds for people's whatevers during a global pandemic. You would have to describe that as a pretty remarkable outcome from all angles. They were just sets, after all: up today, down tomorrow. And yet apparently not. The sheer persistence of these shows, their enduring place in the British imagination, was something that none of us who were involved in the making of them could ever have predicted. The world moves on and much gets left behind, but some shows just seem to move along with it. Even now those shows were offering a place of refuge.

And so was Ronnie Barker, I was delighted to see.

It was soon after the moment in the pandemic where the government, who had formerly been advising us to 'Stay at Home', now felt able to relax the restrictions slightly and amend the slogan to: 'Stay Alert, Control the Virus, Save Lives'. The first portion of that piece of advice drew mockery, not least from people who remembered the moth-eaten old joke that it seemed to be unwittingly reviving: Be Alert – Your Country Needs Lerts.

Still, it was thrown into the shadow by the jingle we were all being encouraged to recite later in the pandemic: 'Hands, Face, Space'. Who writes these things? And is it by any chance the person who came up with the lyric for the children's classic, 'Head, Shoulders, Knees and Toes'? I don't mean to shine my own lapel here, but 'Trigger's broom: We'll beat this soon,' was a work of art by comparison.

Anyway, at some point in the 'Stay Alert, Control the Virus, Save Lives' stage of the pandemic response, some wag put together a photoshopped picture of Ronnie Barker which made him appear to be addressing the nation from behind the podium at one of the government's daily televised coronavirus briefings from Number 10.

Clearly Ronnie's work as arguably our nation's finest ever wielder of spoonerisms and malapropisms was far from forgotten in 2020. The image needed no caption, and no further explanation beyond the slogan emblazoned across the front of the lectern which, in a perfect pastiche of the government's green black and yellow design, read:

'Stale Yurt, Cajole the Walrus, Shave Wives.'

I think Ronnie would have heartily approved of that. Actually, had he still been with us, I think he would have written it.

And he would have struggled with the lockdown as much as I did.

CHAPTER FIVE

On taking to the stage, and on learning on the job.
Plus the life-changing tip I got from Fagin

I told you about that taxi driver who wouldn't accept my offer of free tickets to *No Sex Please, We're British* because he didn't think the theatre was 'for the likes of me'. My parents would have said the same about themselves. Only about eight miles separated the West End from North Finchley, but those theatres might as well have been down around the Antarctic for all that my mother and father would have seen them as somewhere they might go for an evening and feel comfortable. Theatre was not for the likes of them.

My mother, though, would come and see me in amateur dramatic productions. That seemed to be an altogether different proposition. Going to watch your own offspring treading the boards with the Incognito Players up the road at Friern Barnet and venturing out into the world of 'proper' theatre were two entirely unrelated activities, as far as my mother was concerned – one open to her, the other not. My father would come to see me sometimes, too, though not as frequently. He would be too tired after a long day's work. Or that would be his excuse, anyway. Mostly it was my mother, normally accompanied by her sister, my Aunt Ede, with whom she formed a pretty inseparable pairing.

Both of them had left Wales and come to London to get away from their father, someone I generally understood to have been domineering, possibly cruel and almost certainly alcoholic, though none of this was much spoken about in my childhood – a veil of discretion was drawn over this, as over most 'difficult' matters. But my mother came away first, and found a job in service, and her sister followed her and did the same. Both of them spoke Welsh and had barely a word of English when they arrived. They picked it up as they went along. But Ede had found work in a slightly posher household than my mother and her English accent reflected that. She would pronounce 'nuisance' as 'nuance-sense.' 'It's such a *nuance-sense*,' she would say. I guess that was the beginning of me noticing accents and patterns of speech and starting the lifelong business of filing that stuff away for later use.

Unlike the wonderful warm and welcoming cinemas that we enjoyed frequenting in the company of John Wayne, the 'playhouse' of the Incognito Theatre Group lacked the enticement of creature comforts. The Incogs are still going, by the way, on the same premises, and these days they've got themselves a tidy little facility there. (I'm proud to be the company's patron.) But back then, the building was still undeniably a former factory, furnished in the late 1930s with a set of seats from a bombed-out cinema, and its lavatories were outside, down a passageway at the side of the building. Home from home, then. There was no lighting down that passageway, but a torch was provided so that patrons could light their way to relief during the interval. Really, we thought of everything.

The factory had once made lemonade and for a while, at the beginning of the twentieth century, it seems to have been the home of the Barnet Aerated Water Company Ltd, and turned out bottled mineral water. Now there's a coincidence. Some years later, someone I knew well would do a bit in that line of business, too. (You'll probably remember Peckham Spring Water – *Only Fools* Christmas Special, 1992. Water from an ancient natural source. And, as Del says, sources don't get much more natural or ancient than the Thames.)

It was into this slightly makeshift environment that Olwen and Ede would venture to watch 'young David' take his first concerted steps as an actor. And all credit to them for doing so, frankly, because if theatre wasn't your regular idea of a night out, the Incogs didn't necessarily go easy on you. Under the enthusiastic guidance of a man called Doug Weatherhead, the group wasn't shy of grabbing hold of the latest contemporary writing for the stage and having an amateur stab at it.

Thus, in 1957, at the age of seventeen, I found myself playing Cliff Lewis, the Welsh lodger in John Osborne's *Look Back in Anger* – this merely a year after the play had made its ground-breaking and controversial debut at the Royal Court. I'm sure my mother and my aunt enjoyed hearing me honour my lineage by going for the Welsh accent, but I wonder how much else about the grim realism of that production they really enjoyed or felt was 'appropriate'.

Just a couple of months before that, they would have taken their seats to see me in Mordaunt Shairp's *The Green Bay Tree*, a play from the 1930s that subtly explores an implied homosexual relationship between a man and his protégé (me) – a suggestion which, I would hazard, went right over the heads of my mother and Aunt Ede, as, in all honesty, it probably went right over mine, too, at the time. Still, none of this was exactly knockabout stuff. And there weren't all that many laughs to be squeezed, either, from the productions of Henrik Ibsen's *Ghosts* and August Strindberg's *Easter*, which were successively on the Incogs' bill in 1958.

Yet still they loyally came. The following year, we were back on Osborne, doing *Epitaph for George Dillon*, which he wrote in collaboration with Anthony Creighton. A line from that play has stayed with me ever since: 'Life is hard, George, and anyone who thinks it isn't is either very young or a fool. And you're not either.'

Great line, full of truth – but again, of course, not designed to have either your mother or your aunt flopping to the floor with uncontainable mirth.

Then there was the night I appeared to invoke the wrath of God. I don't think that particularly amused the watching members of my family, either. This was when I was performing with the Manor Players, another local north London am-dram group with whom I used to 'moonlight' when not busy with the Incogs. (You will perhaps form the impression that I couldn't get enough of this amateur dramatic stuff in those early years. And you will be right.) One time we were putting on *The Vigil*, a play from 1947 by the Hungarian writer Ladislas Fodor. The venue was a big old church in the suburbs of Finchley. This one was attended by my mother who brought, not Aunt Ede this time, but my younger sister, June, who would probably have been about eleven or twelve.

The Vigil is a great Biblical piece, done as a courtroom drama in which the head gardener at Gethsemane is put on trial, accused of stealing the body of Jesus Christ from the tomb after the crucifixion. The gardener's defence, of course, is that Christ was resurrected – so, nothing to do with him, guv. But it's an enormously dramatic and extremely tense play, asking these big questions and putting various beliefs to the test. My role was the Counsel for the Prosecution and, from memory, I at one point had to call Mary Magdalene to the stand and begin to give her a stern working over.

'I put it to you,' I had to say, in my best uncompromisingly haughty legal style, 'that Jesus Christ was NOT the son of God.'

Mary did not reply, in accordance with the script, and I repeated the question, equally ruthlessly.

'I put it to you again that Jesus Christ was NOT the son of God.'

At this exact moment, outside in the real world, the most enormous crack of thunder broke above the church, shaking the place to its foundations.

Well, as the saying goes: God moves in mysterious ways, his sound effects to perform. You can imagine the impact of this booming intervention from the heavens on the audience – and indeed on the cast, as would no doubt have been evidenced by the laundry basket afterwards. That time I nearly did put my mother on the floor, and my beloved sister along with her. Indeed, I'm not sure June has ever really recovered from that experience.

So, gritty kitchen sink realism, gruelling northern European musings on death and the afterlife, and actual live interventions by a wrathful deity – all of this, I belatedly realise, I inflicted on my supportive mother and other family members during my am-dram days, and all in a medium that wasn't really 'for the likes of them'.

And so I ask myself, as I sit and muse contemplatively in the softly dappled shade beneath the groaning boughs of the towering grapefruit bush: with my background being as it was, how did I end up coming to the conclusion that the theatre was definitely for the likes of me?

Well, there's one simple answer to that: on account of a slightly menacing headmaster.

I've told the story of my abrupt elevation to the stage many times now, but that doesn't mean it gets any easier to tell. It's a tale fraught with peril, as I found out to my cost on *Parkinson* one night.

A brief recap of the basic narrative: with less than a week to curtain up, the leading man in Northside Secondary Modern School's eagerly anticipated 1954 production of *Wayside War* is confined to his bed by a case of the measles. Or was it the mumps? It was one or the other. Hands are thrown upwards among the teaching staff and panic sets in. A stand-in must be found, and quick, or a whole bunch of ticket-holding parents are going to be arriving on the premises on Friday night with no play to see.

The teachers' search for a replacement eventually brings them to your author, then aged fourteen. Your author has no dramatic experience and nor has he ever announced any intention to gain any. However, he has established a small reputation within the school for mimickry, specifically of the teachers. He has also attracted some decent notices for his tireless performance, practically all day long, in the role of would-be 'Jack the Lad'. On the back of those two things, some of the staff seem to have spotted some potential in your author for a leading role in the school play – or, at least, they have come to that conclusion in the face of an extreme and increasingly desperate situation.

The headmaster, a Mr Hackett (possibly well named), eventually corners your author in a corridor and suggests to him that he, the author, steps up to the plate, assumes the vacant leading role and comes to the rescue of the school play and the school's reputation more generally.

Your author, naturally, greets the suggestion with derision, and makes clear his feeling that thespian activities involving dressing up and wearing make-up are well beneath him and absolutely not what anybody who is already appearing daily in the classroom, the playground and the canteen as a would-be Jack the Lad would ever consider putting on his CV. Are you kidding? The potential for reputational damage among all the other already confirmed Jack the Lads was far too great.

Indeed, the author's great school pal, Micky Weedon, is already in the play, a weakness for which he has been earning any amount of merciless stick from your author during the last month. If the author now has to come slinking into the production at this late hour and face the glee of his wounded friend ... well, what a humiliating reversal this would be.

So, basically, sorry Mr Hackett: hate to disappoint you, obviously, but it's a no from me.

To which the headmaster responds by saying, with a steely glint in his eye: 'Don't make me have to tell you to do it.'

In other words: volunteer or be volunteered, pal. We were looking at what Del would no doubt have referred to as a 'fait accompli' – which is slightly better than a 'fait worse than death', but only just.

So, that's the story, and by no means the first time I've found myself uttering it – and yet, blimey, I can find it hard to tell. The headmaster's line, there, with its kind of double, or maybe even triple, imperative going on: that's a slippery customer if you're not careful.

Ripple dissolve, then, to 2007, when I was invited to do an interview on the BBC with Michael Parkinson, whose reputation goes before him, of course, as the great master of the television chat show. So, not an invitation you take lightly, and not an occasion on which you're particularly keen to screw up or find your tongue getting into knots.

Anyway, it was all going pretty well. I had negotiated the stairs onto the set without slipping onto my backside (always a threat that's in your mind at the time, no matter how much of this stuff you've done). I had made it to my seat successfully, shaken hands with my host and sat down without knocking the glasses of water over. Parky had lobbed me a couple of gentle ones to begin with and I had answered them OK and all seemed to be going swimmingly.

It was at that point that Parky asked if he could take me back to my very first appearance on a stage. Well, I relaxed even more at that point, realising that this cued in my *Wayside War* tale, buying me at least a minute and a half of TV interview gold if I played my cards right.

So I set the scene, introduced the measles and the potentially ruinous hole in the cast and my reputation-based refusal to want anything to do with it. And then, in full flow, I got to the bit where the headmaster collared me in the corridor.

' … And he said, "Don't have to make me ask you to do it."'

I paused after that. In my head, I was thinking: that didn't come out quite right, did it? Probably ought to try that again.

I tried it again.

'No … He said, "Don't ask me to … make you to … tell you to … do it."'

Hmm. That didn't quite sound right, either. But maybe it would if I repeated it, but this time a bit faster.

'Don't ask me to make you to tell you to do it … '

Nope. Still didn't sound right. Still didn't make very much sense at all, in fact. It was time to stop digging here, clearly, and time, instead, to find a way to clamber out of this self-manufactured hole before Parky felt he had to take pity and lob me a rope. So I paused again, allowed my brain to whir for a moment, and went for the rescue line.

'By the time the play finished, I still hadn't worked out what he meant.'

And with one bound I was free. The studio audience laughed, to my immense relief, as did Parky, sympathetically, and the moment of my confusion passed.

The lesson being: if in doubt, improvise wildly.

Tripped up by the punchline to your own story, though: that's never a particularly good outcome. Oh, well. It was only *Parkinson* ...

Anyway, the key consequence of that piece of strong-arming by the headmaster was that I ended up figuring prominently in a one-act play by Margaret Napier about espionage in the English Civil War. For this role I was required to don the tricorn hat and elaborately cuffed coat of a seventeenth-century Cavalier. Also a wig of flowing curls. You can imagine how that last detail in particular played with the qualified Jack the Lads in my peer group.

As it happened, though, I rather enjoyed myself. In fact, don't tell Mr Hackett, but I enjoyed myself a lot. Something in me seemed to respond to this experience – the dressing up, the tension, all the excitement beforehand with the audience gathered in the hall and waiting. And

then, of course, the attention – though not on me, specifically, which I would have found profoundly uncomfortable,
but on this character I was required to be for this particular
hour or so. And then, at the end of it all, the applause. I
can't deny that I didn't rather enjoy that as well. I wasn't
used to feeling approved of in the context of school. It was
a whole new sensation.

Not only did that production survive its trial by parental
audience, it was also considered strong enough to compete
in the East Finchley Drama Festival of 1954 where it won
in its category. So the fuss and attention around that, along
with the competitive element which I hadn't realised could
be a part of drama, rather made me look at the whole world
of thespian activity and curly wig-wearing in an even more
attractive light.

And soon after that, the aforementioned Doug Weatherhead was asking me whether I fancied trying out on Monday
nights with the juniors at the Incognito Theatre Group –
and casually, or perhaps very deliberately, mentioning that
they currently had about twenty girls and almost no boys up
there, which certainly got my attention. (It also got the
attention of my pal Micky Weedon, who joined at the same
time as me and for similar motives.) And shortly after that
I was subjecting my mother and my Aunt Ede to two hours
of Strindberg that they never saw coming.

We can decide, with the benefit of retrospect, that our
destinies were all mapped out for us in advance, but it always

looks more like a chain of happenstance to me – and not an especially strong chain, either. I always get an eerie feeling when I look back and do join-the-dots on my past. You just end up realising how fragile everything was at every stage. It would only have taken one of the dots to be in a different place, through no doing of your own, and the picture you would have drawn would have been completely different.

No measles, no menacing headmaster; no menacing headmaster, no *Wayside War*; no *Wayside War*, no victory in that drama festival; no victory in that drama festival, no approach from Doug Weatherhead to join the Incogs; no Incogs, no notion of ever becoming a professional actor. How easy it would have been for the chain to separate and fall to bits at any point along the way.

There was still a huge leap to make, of course, between knocking about in amateur productions in my spare evenings and deciding that this was a plausible career for me – something to consider 'a living'. Again, I remain a little nonplussed about how I summoned the confidence to make that leap. Part of it was that people who saw me in those am-dram shows kept telling me I should do it. When you start to hear positive feedback from others, it definitely emboldens you. I even remember someone floating the idea of me applying to drama school – not a notion I had considered up to that point. It was at a drama festival of some description where I had performed and done quite well, and someone from the council, who I think was on the judging panel, gave me a nudge afterwards and said she thought a drama school would probably look quite kindly on an application from me and that I could probably get a grant to cover the cost of it, if I needed one, which I would have done.

I also remember mentioning this conversation soon after to my parents and neither of them being especially impressed with the idea. But maybe I wasn't all that impressed with it myself, either, deep down. I certainly didn't pursue the scheme with any vigour, which would suggest it had merely intrigued me as a prospect rather than grabbed me by the lapels.

And no wonder, really. I would have been about twenty-two at the time. I was out in the big wide world, earning my keep and dutifully peeling off some of my meagre earnings to hand my mum to pay my way at home. I had a job, I had a little bit of money in my pocket and I had the firm's second-hand van – all of which put me well on the way to, if not international jet-set pleasure, then to jet-set pleasure North Finchley style. Becoming a student at that point in the journey would have seemed like a big step backwards.

It's also true, I think, that, at that point, the theatre had only really begun to dig her claws into me and draw me into her embrace. It would be another couple of years before she drew me in completely, and by then drama school would be well out of the picture.

Would drama school even have suited me? I wasn't a good student, nor particularly well adjusted to an academic environment. I think the teachers who taught me at Northside Secondary Modern and who regularly noted my position – third from bottom of the class in most subjects – would happily have confirmed that. And the teachers at Enfield Technical College when I was on day release would probably also have testified to a certain, shall we say, restlessness on my part within the confines of the classroom.

Learning on the job, though – that seemed to be something I could find the motivation and the application to do. And learning on the job was how I became an actor. Everything that drama school might have taught me about timing and projecting my voice and using gestures and occupying the stage space, I had to learn by getting myself into productions and onto stages in any way that I could and seeing what happened.

As it turned out, having a trade would prove extremely useful. Even after I had clinched my first paying job in rep, down at the Bromley Theatre in south London, acting would remain precarious for a little while. There was no guarantee of a steady flow of work – that would only come later. When I decided to take the plunge to see if I could make it as a professional, I handed over my share in our electrical business to my good friend and partner Bob Bevil in exchange for one of our two minivans, but also in the knowledge that Bob would take me on for shifts here and there when the acting went thin – which frequently happened, of course, as I scrabbled to get myself going and establish myself.

Indeed, that wasn't the only work I ended up having to take on to patch over the gaps. There was a guy I was introduced to called Peter Davey, a jobbing actor who had been married to Anna Wing, the actor who would eventually play Lou Beale, the matriarch of the Beale family, in *East-Enders*. Peter brought an entrepreneurial spirit to the problem of 'periodic unemployment' that beset our industry. For a while he was doubling as a door-to-door salesman for Encyclopaedia Britannica, carting a suitcase around, pushing doorbells and trying to flog the famous multi-volume fount of all knowledge (no properly aspiring home complete without one).

But when that stopped working for him, Peter set up a company called Ideal Home, possibly inviting a legal confrontation with the famous magazine of the same name, but no matter. Ideal Home was basically a one-stop-shop for all your home maintenance needs. If you wanted a fence fixed or a dripping tap tightened or a room re-decorated, and you were in the London area, you called Ideal Home and Peter would have one of his network of qualified workmen round to you in no time – that network of qualified workmen being exclusively made up from the ranks of currently unemployed actors, including, from time to time, yours truly.

When I was, as actors like to say, 'resting' – or, to use the gentler American term, 'reading' – I would ring up Peter to see what he had on the books, and he would say, 'How are your painting and decorating skills?' And I would reply, 'Top of the range, Peter,' while actually thinking to myself, 'Hmm, pretty average, if we're being honest.' And the next thing, I would be slapping the Dulux on somebody's bathroom wall.

Gutter clearance was another belatedly discovered expertise of mine. Peter seemed to attract a lot of custom from people with clogged guttering, and I never minded being assigned to the task. Indeed, by comparison with dragging electrical wiring around in the dusty, mice-infested cavities under floorboards, gutter clearance was a real breath of fresh air.

All in all, the Ideal Home set-up seemed like a perfect solution at the time, although, of course, it was sobering for someone just starting out to observe that a lot of actors on the ring-around list seemed to be doing far more painting and decorating than they were doing acting. But we all needed a fall-back, and for a while there, Peter very usefully supplied one.

Of course, it wasn't just actors who muddled along in this way, waiting for the golden path of opportunity to open up. John Sullivan, the writer of *Only Fools*, took on all sorts of odd jobs to keep himself going while he was trying to come through as a writer. One of those jobs was window-cleaning and John used to tell a story of being up a ladder and seeing, through the window he was cleaning, something he had written going out on the television. A pure George Formby moment for John, that. Writers knew as well as actors the great truth that a break here and there didn't necessarily catapult you direct to the promised land where you were free to concentrate on your chosen craft.

So for me in those early days, it was a life of contrasts, you might say. One moment I was applying the grease-paint and wowing the people of Bromley with my, if I may say, exquisitely well-observed portrayal of a hotel porter in the farce *Diplomatic Baggage*; and the next day I was up a ladder with a fistful of wet leaves. But you'd say one thing for going that way about it: it kept you grounded. It's very hard to get fancy ideas about yourself as an 'artiste' when you're moving effortlessly from Restoration costume to paint-spattered boiler-suit and back again.

It also meant I ended up forming a pretty robust attitude to acting: that it might not be as physically demanding as hard manual labour and that it might not be what a lot of people would consider 'work'. But nevertheless, if you were privileged enough to occupy yourself this way, it was your duty to treat it as a job, like any other. Roll up your sleeves, get your hands dirty, do the work. I'm not sure I would have had the same kind of practical attitude to it if I had come out of college.

The lesson being: there is more than one way to skin a cat. And none of them is going be that pleasurable for the cat.

I certainly don't regret not going to drama school, then – except perhaps in one small regard. Those of us who are self-taught end up carrying it with us a bit, I think. If you have gone about things your own way, you have a strong sense, at the back of your mind, that there was a 'proper' way to have gone about those things which you somehow skipped. It's not exactly that you feel you've cheated the system or come by something that wasn't your due: the chances are you have had to work as hard, or even harder, than people who have come through the 'proper' way. It's just that you can't help wondering from time to time what you missed and whether the 'proper' way is going to creep up and trip you up one day.

And you certainly worry a lot about what people who did go about it the 'proper' way might be thinking about you and the way you do things. You have a feeling sometimes that you're waiting to be found out.

So, to class anxiety, I could now add education anxiety. One more anxiety and I would be able to jump out of my seat and shout, 'House!' But it's one of the very few things I would change if I were able to go back. I would like to have found the strength from somewhere to be a bit bolder about shutting off that little nagging voice when it started up about my lack of formal training – to have risen above the insecurity and learned to ignore it, or even forced it to go away. I could have saved myself a lot of unnecessary worry. And it *was* unnecessary – I know that now.

If you're learning on the job, you're going to need good people around you. And I was extremely fortunate in some of the people I was able to learn from. I intend to pick each of them out as we go through this book, and explain what they offered me, but let me start with someone I met in late 1966, in the days when I was a pirate.

This was the opening period of my career when I was getting hold of the industry newspaper, *The Stage*, turning to the ads at the back of it and ringing up or writing away for everything that was going. And mostly I was hearing silence and occasionally I was getting invited to audition and then hearing silence. But I was sticking at it, and sometimes I was striking lucky and getting some actual work to do. And one such occasion was when I was given a small role as the Gentleman Starkey in a production of *Peter Pan*, set to run for three weeks at the Scala Theatre on Charlotte Street (a lovely old Victorian venue but, alas, long since demolished and replaced with offices) and then to go on tour around the UK after that. Among us smaller part players at that time, there was a saying that went: 'There are no small parts, only small actors.' Well, I certainly fitted the bill there.

Perhaps you're thinking: ah, panto, then. And, yes, I guess this was indeed a musical Christmas entertainment, but as pantomime goes, it was very superior. It was a big, well-worked production with an expensive and beautifully constructed set and a properly starry cast. Playing Peter Pan was Julia Lockwood, who was the daughter of British film royalty (Margaret Lockwood) and had been a star since childhood. And in the role of Captain Hook was the great Ron Moody.

For us bit-part players, there was not to be much interaction with Julia Lockwood, much as we would have longed for it. Mostly we were reduced to smiling bashfully and pressing our backs against the walls of the corridor as, accompanied by her assistant and trailing glamour and charisma, the star of the show floated into the theatre and closeted herself away behind the door of the Number One dressing room.

Your own dressing room! With your name on the door! Those were unthinkable glories. Of course, twelve years later, a Number One dressing room would be reserved for me when I was in *No Sex Please*, and it would be *me* floating into a theatre and trailing glamour and charisma – or after a fashion anyway. But it was a prospect I would have found hard to imagine during that week in 1966, as I meekly shuffled past on my way to the stage in my pirate costume, hoping to be favoured with even a passing glance from Miss Lockwood's beautiful eyes or (blessing of blessings) a 'good evening'.

I also would have found it hard to imagine how unglamorous that dressing room probably was, in fact, when you got on the other side of the door. If it was like the Number One dressing room at the Strand, it was a pokey place with exposed pipes all over the place and sorely in need of a lick of paint. But that's theatre, folks. (And with all that painting and decorating talent going to waste in the business, too.)

Ron Moody, on the other hand, was a far more approachable figure. He was still two years away from playing the definitive Fagin in Carol Reed's film adaptation of *Oliver!* and becoming a household name for it. (In my humble opinion, Ron Moody doing 'Reviewing the Situation' from *Oliver!* may be about as perfect as musical numbers get, an absolute object lesson in expression and gesture and control.) But even at this point he was already a big star, having played that role for a year in the original stage production. When the production eventually rolled out onto the road, Ron and Julia would be staying in decent hotels, while we more lowly cast members had to seek out digs for ourselves, a ritual I would get used to. Nonetheless, Ron was a team player who erected no barriers around himself. After shows, he would happily join, and even lead, the cast's march on the nearest curry house. So imagine the thrill for a young unknown actor of finding himself out for a curry with Ron Moody, sitting there in awe while Ron, who was a tremendous raconteur and a brilliant mimic, held forth over the poppadoms.

Imagine the value, also, of being able to watch Ron Moody work from a position up close. Those weeks in London and on the road were an education for me. Ron's first professional engagements were in cabaret, and cabaret clearly taught him to love audiences – specifically to love the sense he had of *contact* with the audience. He hated to pretend that the audience wasn't there, which is, of course, the standard conceit in the theatre. The audience, conventionally, sits shrouded in the dark and the actors on the stage studiously ignore them.

Not so with Ron, who, as he bounded about the stage in that *Peter Pan*, seemed to be seeking the audience out with his eyes, peering through the glare of the lights, looking for a connection. It was also clear that the script was by no means sacred to him: if he could find an ad lib, or something to tease out for an extra laugh, he would do so. I'm not sure how completely this enamoured him to Julia Lockwood and other members of the cast, who kept finding the rules of engagement changing every night. But I do know that it made for a hell of a show.

I had a particular problem during that production that I was eventually moved to consult Ron about. And he gave me some advice that opened my eyes. It all stemmed from a moment in the show when I had to go out and do a brief front-of-curtain piece with Leslie Sarony, of The Two Leslies, who were very big in the days before my time. This moment was a bit of extraneous business to buy time while the set was being switched behind the scenes. Obviously that was a brilliant opportunity, in principle – a chance to occupy the stage with this great man who was playing Smee and to have the attention of the audience fully on the pair of us. Oh yes, and also, I now remember, on a giant prop crocodile. But it didn't turn out to be so brilliant in practice. The exact content of this little diversionary act has now escaped my memory – or maybe I have deliberately suppressed that memory down the years, because the moment was truly a stinker. There was nothing there for the audience to laugh at and every night we would go out there and die an absolute death. Waves of indifference would wash up from the audience and we would exit feeling like a pair of complete and utter prawns.

As soon as this started happening, I talked to the director about getting the moment changed, or injecting something else in there – anything to awaken the audience from the torpor that they were descending into for those pancake-flat moments.

But the director was insistent. He told me to stick with it. It was funny, he seemed to be suggesting: people just didn't realise it yet. Give it a bit longer and they would start coming around. That was the script and we should just carry on with it – it was all fine.

I didn't quite follow the logic there. But back we went, and stuck at it. And the moment didn't magically get any better and we continued to die on our backsides on a nightly basis. The situation was spoiling the whole show for me. Even though the rest of the night was great fun, I always had this front-of-curtain moment in the back of my mind, causing me dread, and that's a horrible position to be in when you're in the middle of a show.

Eventually, backstage one day, I talked to Ron Moody about it. I told him I was unhappy with this bit of the show and that I was sure there were better ways to do it, but that the director was keeping me in check. Ron gave me a level look.

'Well, who are you going to trust?' he said. 'The director or the audience?'

In some ways, that was something only a big star could say out loud. Questioning the authority of the director? What kind of fearless insubordination was this? For a new-comer to the business, still wet behind the ears, this was a breathtaking and even quite thrilling thing to hear. The smoke of rebellion was in the air!

So, duly emboldened, I went straight back out there, did my own thing in that little slot regardless, and knocked them dead every night for the remainder of the run.

OK, not really. I was way too new to the game to be acting like that. Yet the clarity of Ron's words did stay with me. They cut to the chase and pointed to a very important truth – and, of course, the best directors know it, too. Ultimately, in entertainment, when it comes to working out whether something works or not, there is no better or less fallible judge than the audience. I definitely took that forward with me.

Long after this, Ron would continue to be someone whose approach to things I continued to think about and respect. He was known, of course, for playing Fagin, but absolutely determined not to get stuck with that and type-cast for the rest of his career. He had the guts to leave the stage version of *Oliver!* after a year and not to travel with it to America because he felt he had done all he wanted to do in the stage role. I would have some struggles of my own with typecasting along the way, as we shall see, and would only come to admire Ron's strength in that area even more fully.

He was courageous enough to turn things down if he felt they didn't suit him. Indeed, he almost turned down Fagin, it seems, but was eventually pushed into it by his agent after two others had declined the role. And he turned down *Doctor Who*, after Patrick Troughton stood down. That was an especially bold move. Jon Pertwee took on the role at that point, and I don't suppose he ever regretted doing so. Was Ron Moody the best Doctor Who we never had? It wouldn't be an idle assertion.

Ron thought he was better off writing musicals than per-forming, in which assumption people tended to say he was misguided – except that that was what he wanted to do, so why not? He had the fantastic self-confidence of someone who thoroughly knew his own mind. That, too, was inspi-rational for me, watching him over those curries and on

Long before the aid of computers, this was my first professional photograph, taken around 1965, which I circulated to any prospective producer.

I've known this grapefruit tree since it was a pip, and now here it is, still with me, half a century later. The moral of this story is that if you take an unpromising little seed and patiently water it, then eventually it will get so big that you'll put your back out trying to drag the damn thing outside.

Above left: Here I am with Rob Knights, the director of *Porterhouse Blue*, on a location mocked up to look like the University of Cambridge where my character Skullion was Head Porter.

Above right: Here I am reminiscing with my good friend Humphrey Barclay, who first discovered me on Bournemouth Pier and someone who, since then, I have worked together with many times.

Comical elderliness? That was one of my earliest calling cards as an actor, right from the first time, in 1969, that Ronnie B asked me to play Dithers (see illustration, painted by Humphrey Barclay), the spectacularly dessicated yet somehow still upright 100-year-old gardener that Ronnie created for *Hark at Barker* and later for *His Lordship Entertains*.

Top left: ITV gave Denise Coffey and I a children's show called *Two D's and a Dog*. We played a couple of youthful amateur crime-fighters and mystery sleuths. Think *Scooby Doo*, but without the animation. We did, however, have a dog. (*Shutterstock/Fremantle Media*)

Top right: The first time my name appeared in lights for *Look No Hans* in 1985. I had the lead role as Peter Fisher, a British car salesman working in Berlin and doubling as a fumbling undercover agent. Look, I didn't say it was Shakespeare, did I? And my co-star Anita Graham would have known: she was a former RSC actor.

In *Cinderella*, 1979 in Newcastle, with Leah Bell. I am Buttons, and Buttons – correct me if I'm wrong here – is one of those roles (Lear and Hamlet are others) by which an actor comes to judge himself. (*Getty/Mirrorpix*)

Me and the cast for 'The Jolly Boys' Outing', the eighth Christmas special episode of *Only Fools and Horses*, Christmas 1989.

I used to think it was so clever of *Only Fools* creator John Sullivan to have created a company name, Trotters Independent Trading, which, as well as being just a touch too grand for itself, would produce the deflating acronym 'TIT' on its headed notepaper – until, that is, John confessed that he hadn't realised it would do so himself. Can you believe that? The lesson being: you don't always know when you're making a TIT of yourself. (*Getty/Radio Times*)

On the set of *Still Open All Hours* with my co-star, James Baxter. For me, Granville and Del are chalk and cheese. Granville always looks weary with the cards that life has dealt him, while Del is always going to play his hand, whatever feeble cards fate has put in it.

Me with John Challis (aka Boycie) and *Only Fools and Horses* director Anthony 'Tony' Dow in front of some choice Del Boy graffiti in Margate.

A signed keepsake from one of my favourite special episodes of *Only Fools and Horses*, 'Beckham in Peckham', filmed in aid of Sport Relief in 2014. The episode ends with Beckham dramatically falling over as he tries to lean back against a goods cart that, at the crucial moment, gets moved away! It's not quite my falling through the bar flap, but old Golden Balls had a jolly good crack at it.

On the first day of the David Jason exhibition, a familiar figure suddenly plonked himself down on the chair bedside me, smiled broadly and reached for my hand. Blimey, I thought: this bloke's a dead ringer for Ricky Hatton, the boxer. And it was Ricky Hatton, the boxer.

What an iconic vehicle this has become!

Comedy royalty. Ronnie Corbett once noticed that, in an entire season of shows at the London Palladium, Ronnie Barker worked so precisely that even his hand gestures were the same, show after show. He made it look natural, but it was anything but. It was the product of hard study. Perhaps most important of all, he taught me to respect the fact that absolutely everybody involved in a show contributes to that show's success. Ronnie C and I presented a BAFTA Fellowship Award to Ronnie B on this special night, at the BBC Television Centre.

Obviously being a knight of the realm (an honour bestowed upon me in 2005) comes with its perks. Automatic upgrades on aeroplanes, the best rooms in hotels and triple Nectar points – not so much. More day dreams, I'm afraid, but you do get invited to choose yourself a coat of arms. I'm now the proud bearer – or at least my wall is – of the famous Sir David John White OBE coat of arms (my real name, in case you didn't know). Not bad, coming from my humble beginnings.

Top left: My wonderful wife Gill and I in our glad rags.

Top right: At 'The Firm', receiving my knighthood for services to acting, with Gill and my daughter, Sophie. Sophie has never forgiven the Queen for not letting her in to the ceremony, as she was too young to sit through the presentation. Her grandma brought her for the photographs, though.

Sophie looking all grown-up and beautiful. In January 2020, when our part of the world was still free to gather together in blissful pre-Covid ease, I went with Gill and Sophie to the premiere of the Cirque du Soleil show *Luzia* at the Royal Albert Hall. Pretty good, thank you for asking. I love a Cirque du Soleil show; so much so, in fact, that I'll even run the gamut of the dreaded red carpet, showing my best side to the cameras. (*Getty/Dave J Hogan*)

that stage. I would never have that confidence to anything like the extent that he had it, but I would fight for my share of it when I had to, and I would often think of Ron Moody when I was doing so.

CHAPTER SIX

*On my reconciliation with Del, and on
finally gathering with the faithful*

A couple of weeks after my birthday, with the bountiful congratulations of a joyous nation still ringing in my ears, and with the bunting finally and reluctantly coming down and getting packed away after the street parties around the country, I found myself in a hotel banqueting and conference suite near Bedford, signing car parts.

Not just any hotel banqueting and conference suite, I should add: 'one of Bedfordshire's premier banqueting and conference suites,' according to no less a judge of this kind of thing than the place's own website.

And not just any car parts, either. Bits of yellow Reliant Regal of the sort driven by ... well, you probably know which independent trading company had one of those as its mode of transport.

Incidentally, I used to think it was so clever of John Sullivan to have created a company name, Trotters Independent Trading, which, as well as being just a touch too grand for itself, would produce the deflating acronym 'TIT' on its headed notepaper – until, that is, John confessed that he hadn't realised it would do so himself until much later, when he saw the acronym written down. Can you believe that it never occurred to him, apparently? Purest serendipity, like many of the best things in comedy.

The lesson being: you don't always know when you're making a TIT of yourself.

Anyway, there I was, on a Saturday morning, in a Bedford conference suite with a black marker pen in hand, adding my name to a small selection of yellow replica Regal panels, doors and bumpers, which seem to go a bomb as keepsakes and ornaments in the homes of the more discerning kind of *Only Fools and Horses* fans.

And as well as adding my name to these prized items, I was also receiving requests to dedicate those car parts. And what that meant, in turn, was that I at one point found myself being asked to use my pen to write, around the rim of a replica of the Reliant's back door, the legend: 'Shut up you tart!! David Jason.' I bet Tom Cruise doesn't sign like that. When I next meet him on a film set somewhere, I'll ask him.

I am reminded of the story that the writer Alan Bennett tells about doing a book-signing event, and asking a young man whether he would like him to add any particular message to his signature in the front of the book. The young man said yes, he certainly would like that. And so the author found himself writing: 'Dear Christine, sorry about last night. Love, Alan Bennett.'

Bennett reasoned that the bloke had bought a book so he was entitled to have anything written in it that he wanted. Good for him. And I don't mind saying I feel exactly the same way about people and their car parts. So, 'Shut up you tart!! David Jason' it was, and in my own fair hand. (Apologies, of course, to the tart concerned. It really was nothing personal.)

Meanwhile, around me in the room as I wielded my pen, moved a throng of people of all ages, sizes, sexes, callings and backgrounds, all enthusiastically congregating. Despite the fact that it was a prematurely warm and spring-like day outside, and perfectly balmy inside of course, some of those present wore thick, cable-knit cream-coloured polo-neck jumpers with sheepskin coats and Burberry print flat caps. Others were in T-shirts marked with the simple message: 'Plonker!'

Hoodies, similarly adorned, were available for purchase from a stall, positively groaning with themed merchandise: baseball caps emblazoned with the motto 'Lovely Jubbly', Mandela House signs, playing cards ('That's not the hand I dealt you'), Monopoly sets with pictures of me in a Batman outfit on them, and doormats expressing the touching thought: 'Not farewell – just bonjour.'

It was tempting to imagine what someone would have made of this carnival scene had they been beamed down into the middle of it from a country in which *Only Fools and Horses* had no currency (and, incredible to relate, there are a few of those, although it seems from my own explorations that you can count them on the fingers of one hand). I hazard that such a person would have been a touch confused.

Everyone who was there, of course, knew exactly what the score was, and barely registered a flicker as people dressed as Derek Trotter strolled the floor with car doors tucked under their arms or thoughtfully considered the purchase of a sweatshirt saying, 'All right, Dave?' Possibly they themselves were on their way to the stall where you could get a commemorative photograph of yourself peeping from the back of the Trotters' van in the company of an inflatable sex doll. Or perhaps they were headed to the area where you could ascend a step ladder with a sheet and be snapped re-enacting the chandelier scene. Again, our visitor from abroad would have been shaking their head, one imagines. Sex dolls in van windows? Chandelier scene?

But no such confusion at the annual *Only Fools and Horses* fan convention, which had been slightly tweaked for

2020, the year of my big birthday, to become the home for a 'Sir David Jason Exhibition', in honour of my [*author coughs gently and straightens an invisible tie*] humble career more broadly. And hats off – or rather, hoods off – in this regard to the conventioneer who went the extra mile and turned up dressed as Danger Mouse, which, I have to say, gladdened my heart. One brave crime-fighting mouse in a room full of Dels.

The first *Only Fools* fan convention was in 1998, when the show was still going, and it has become something of an institution and a fixture in the diary. Well, in some people's diaries. Because the truth is, there has been at least one convention every year since then, in various locations around the country. And every year, without fail, as regular as clockwork ... I have not attended it.

It wasn't for the want of an invitation. Perry Aghajanoff is the man responsible for the *Only Fools and Horses* Appreciation Society and the organising force behind these large-scale fan get-togethers. He is also, incidentally, the man with what is indisputably the biggest collection of *Only Fools* memorabilia in captivity, an extraordinary assembly of gear, enough to stock an entire museum dedicated to the show's history, and ranging from original scripts to costumes and props, and extending from an authentic copy of Jumbo Mills' business card all the way out to the actual funnel off the actual *Inge*, the battered old boat on which Del, Rodney and Albert set sale for Holland in 'To Hull and Back'.

Indeed, if you want to see the cardboard box originally used to stage the 'Name the Baby' sweepstake in the Nag's Head, complete with allegedly original handwritten sign and seemingly wrapped in its original Sellotape, Perry is your person. How has he come by this stuff? I consider it wisest to ask no questions in this area, but simply to admire the man's resourcefulness and dedication to the cause.

Perry, with unflagging enthusiasm, has extended an offer to me to join him and all the other guests and fans at the *Only Fools* convention on what must have been (I don't think I'm wrong in saying) an annual basis since the event was founded. And I, with equally unflagging enthusiasm, and on an equally annual basis, have said thank you very much for asking, but if it's OK with you I would rather not.

Now, more often than not, to be fair to myself, I've had a legitimate excuse – off shooting something, busy with work, and so on. But on other occasions, I haven't found the offer hard to resist, if I'm being perfectly honest. Indeed, I'm willing to admit that something in me has historically tended to turn a little cool at the suggestion. Does that sound ungrateful? A little ungracious towards the people in the Del-style jumpers and sheepskins? It's certainly not meant to. Put it down in part to my habitual reluctance to want to appear in places as myself without the comfort of a role to conceal myself in and the security of a script to speak.

In any case, that whole idea of celebrities 'making an appearance' always seems such a baffling one to me. Doing a performance, I understand: but making an appearance? Just showing up and somehow gracing the room with your golden presence? What kind of human interaction is that? And what does that say about where you think you sit, vis-à-vis your fellow beings? 'Please be in awe, if you would, while I deign to appear before you.' The very notion of that, once you pick away at the surface of it a bit, makes me feel so awkward and self-conscious that my toes start to curl up.

Then multiply that reluctance by at least a hundred in places where people might be expecting me to turn up and somehow casually represent Del. Now, just to be clear, for all that Derek Trotter and I undeniably share many physical characteristics, we're altogether different people, when push comes to shove. I don't talk like Del: I have a London accent, in keeping with the place what I was brung up in. But my voice has nowhere near as broad a cockney twang to it as Del's does. I don't move like Del: I don't tend to be flexing my neck and rolling my shoulders to indicate my ongoing stature as a top geezer about town. And the only occasions when I have come out with the kinds of things that Del says have been where there was a John Sullivan script to hand.

Oh, and I don't tend to drive a Reliant Regal unless I really have to, either. I prefer something a little more comfortable over the longer journey, if it's all right with you. I think at my age I'm entitled to that.

All of which, down the years, has slightly complicated the circumstances where people have invited me to things in the hope that Del would show up. Derek Trotter's reputation goes before him, and he's quite a bit to live up to, all things considered. I knew people in the main were perfectly capable of making a separation between the two of us, but nevertheless I would always be worried about disappointing them from the off, because how could I not?

'Here, I met that Del Boy the other day, and do you know what? Huge let-down. Didn't sound like him, didn't dress like him, and he didn't call me a plonker so much as once. Worse than that, he didn't even try to flog me anything in an amusing way that ended up hilariously rebounding on him in a highly amusing denouement roughly forty minutes later.'

On top of all this, there's the fact that my own personal relationship with Derek Trotter down the years has not always been, shall we say, straightforward. Don't get me wrong: I love Del. I feel I know him pretty well by now – almost as well as I know myself, frankly – and I've got an awful lot of time for the bloke. I think I can genuinely say that I would do almost anything to help him if he was in trouble (which most of the time he has been), and I can't begin to express how glad I am that I met him. He was the part of a lifetime. Playing him brought so much into my life, and I'll always be aware of how much I owe him. It's at least a tenner. Plus interest. So let's call it quits at £7.50.

Yet have there been moments, however brief, when ... not that I wished we had never met; that would be far too strong. But moments when I thought the two of us might be getting a bit too close for comfort – where I felt it might be a good idea to try and put some distance between us, if I possibly could. To cool our relationship, you might say. Or, in the modern parlance, to give each other some space for a while.

Permit me to explain. Others may want to knock me back for this, but I'm going to go out on a limb here and suggest that nothing embeds itself in British culture quite like a successful television sitcom. Find yourself in a successful sitcom, one that has really carried some big audiences with it, as *Only Fools* did, and nobody will ever forget you for it. I'm sure the stars of *Dad's Army*, *Are You Being Served?*, *Last of the Summer Wine* and countless others would amply back me up here – those of them who are still standing, of course.

I don't think any of us in the cast was quite ready for the kind of fame that would descend on us as a result of appearing in *Only Fools*. Indeed, how could we have been? Its success was utterly unpredictable. And I think all of us ended up having to adapt to it in our own ways.

When a show starts to engage with people and begins to take an audience along with it, it's an extraordinary thing to find yourself caught up in. You can actually feel the heat around the programme beginning to intensify. The first inkling you get of it is when complete strangers start repeating the show back to you in the street. It's fantastic, of course, especially at the very beginning, when it catches you by surprise and provides you with your first indication that the show is beginning to plant itself in people's imaginations. I suppose the equivalent for singers must be when they see the audience singing along, word-perfect, to one of their songs. You have to think: blimey, people really have been paying some attention here.

But then, in the case of *Only Fools*, it began to build. A few things started to happen that pulled me up slightly and made me think, 'Hang on a moment, something a bit different is going on here.' I noticed, for instance, how pictures of me in the paper were suddenly being captioned, not 'David Jason', but 'Derek Trotter' or 'Del' or 'Del Boy'. A profile of me in one of the broadsheets, which talked about my career in general and used a photograph of me as I am, and not in costume or character as Del, had the headline 'A Del of a Way to Make a Living'. That, too, brought me up short – like an association was now automatically being made that hadn't existed before.

Meanwhile you couldn't help noticing how people were coming at you more and more with the show's catchphrases and greeting you, straight away, as Del, as if the barrier between you and the character had completely melted.

'Oi, Del,' people would come up and say to me, straight off the bat. 'Where's Rodney?'

It was like a version of identity theft. Had I disappeared or something?

'Rodney!' people would call out to Nick Lyndhurst. 'You plonker!' They meant it in the nicest possible way, of course. But it was still quite something to hear, and, for Nick, quite some reaction to generate simply by walking up the road to the shops for a paper.

'All right, Dave?' The late and great Roger Lloyd-Pack used to hear that line of his coming back at him constantly, and in the obscurest places – including, he once avowed, from a stranger walking the other way in the middle of a raging blizzard in Iceland, late at night, when Roger was wearing an anorak with the hood up. 'All right, Dave,' said this Icelandic stranger as he passed and headed on into the night.

Roger came to the conclusion that one day he would climb the highest mountain in Tibet to seek the meaning of life from a cave-dwelling guru up there, and as he eased his exhausted body over the final rocky outcrop and scrambled onto the ledge where the master of all meaningful knowledge sat cross-legged, the guru would say to him, 'All right, Dave?'

Perhaps, of all of us, Lennard Pearce, who played Grandad, enjoyed the change most. Lennard was coming to the end of a good career as a theatre actor. He hadn't been expecting to come by a big TV role and find himself propelled to national fame any time soon. When it happened, he was delighted. The attention in the streets and in the shops, all the autograph-seekers and well-wishers, coming so suddenly at that particular point in his life, seemed to bring him a lot of pleasure and he lapped it up. Would that it had lasted longer for him.

For the rest of us, however, there was a process of adjustment to be made, no question. It's very hard to explain, but it's a little bit as though you have pulled a face and then the wind has changed and, just like your parents warned you that it would when you were a kid, your face has stayed that way. And no matter where you go or what you do, people only see the character you were playing when the wind changed.

My tactic was to wrap myself up in baseball caps and scarves when I went out. Nick Lyndhurst did the same. Roger Lloyd-Pack took to wearing a beaten-up Trilby. None of these disguises really seemed to work. The characters seemed to come peeping out from under them.

'Excuse me – it's you, isn't it? It is! It's Del! I thought I recognised you! Everyone! It's Del over here!'

Eventually, it started to seem a bit inescapable, and a little bit suffocating and – I probably don't need to add – slightly troubling on account of that. I don't mean that people were ever anything other than kind and well-meaning. Indeed, I soon found myself in the extraordinary position of being in a show that people only ever seemed to want to praise. Has anybody come up to me in this whole time and said, 'That *Only Fools* show – that was a bit over-rated, wasn't it? Not too many laughs in that one, were there?' It simply hasn't happened. How rare must that be?

By 'troubling', I simply mean that it was alarming from a professional point of view. Because in the back of your mind, you were thinking: what does this actually mean for the way people see you from now on? Suddenly this one character that you had developed and played for the specific purposes of a television show started coming with you wherever you went. When you walked in, so did he. You didn't have to be wearing his clothes, or speaking his lines or even talking in his accent – he was still there, sitting right in your seat. You couldn't seem to shake him off for love or money.

I know each of us in *Only Fools* had a worrying little moment, somewhere along the line, where we found ourselves wondering: is that it, then? Am I Del Boy for ever now? Or Boycie, or Trigger, or Rodney … ?

Again, no major complaints here: everyone should be so fortunate as to be in a show that goes over as well as *Only Fools*. It's a very wonderful and very privileged bubble to be in. But if what you are hoping to see yourself as is a character actor – a person of many parts, not just one – then it's a bubble you are going to need to emerge from at some point. And you're going to need to protect yourself from some of its effects. If people only see you as Del, then pretty soon casting directors would only be seeing you as Del, too. It was all too easy to imagine the conversations that would then occur in the places where work was getting handed out.

'What about David Jason for this role?'

'What – Del Boy? In the part of the High Commissioner to India, circa 1855? I don't think that would be quite appropriate, would it?'

I had to manage it carefully because otherwise I could envisage a situation in which I would never get another job – except, of course, as a plucky south London wheeler-dealer. And, indeed, as it happened, Del did cost me a few pieces of work along the way and, in other cases, I had to fight really hard just to be able to get into the room and start persuading people that there was more to me than a south London wheeler-dealer, honest, guv. I'll talk about some of those fights in due course.

In the meantime, though, it seemed to me that one of the simplest ways I could manage this unusual predicament was by being careful about the things I said 'yes' to. Invitations to go along and play up the legend of Del, therefore further encouraging people to think of me as that one person only, were invitations that I decided to be wary of, in my better and longer-term interests. Hence no going along to things dressed in costume as Del, which I have been asked to do a lot.

And hence no fan conventions. Strictly none of those.

So now flash forward to 2020 and a certain hotel banqueting suite in Bedfordshire, and here I am at an *Only Fools and Horses* convention – yes, one modified to become a 'David Jason Exhibition', but, let's face it, this is an *OFAH* convention in every regard that matters.

How has this come to pass? Is it possible that I'm getting soft in my old age? Well, I suppose it would follow. As Dudley Moore once said on the topic of growing old: 'What should be soft is hard, and what should be hard is soft.'

I loved Dudley Moore, by the way, whom I came across in the early 1960s and whom I first went to see in the *Beyond the Fringe* revue at the Cambridge Theatre – a show also containing the aforementioned Alan Bennett, of course, not to mention Jonathan Miller and Peter Cook. But it was Dudley Moore, among that distinguished and clever gang, who stood out for me. He was hilariously funny; he didn't seem to be capable of taking himself seriously and he had that irrepressible and highly engaging look of someone who was permanently on the verge of bursting out laughing. He was one of those performers who could make you feel good inside, just by walking out onto a stage and showing his face. There were powers there that I could only dream of. And he was short. For some reason – can't think why – I found that comforting and inspiring back then.

Anyway, hardness becoming soft, the Dudley Moore theory: does that explain why I finally set aside my long-held principles and went to Bedfordshire? (I don't mean I had principles about going to Bedfordshire ... You know what I mean.) I'm not sure the Moore theory exactly applies in this case, though obviously I would be willing to listen to the views of other experts in this area. At the same time, I am sure that being a person of my new-found maturity had at least *something* to do with my change of heart. Because there's no question that the arrival of that big, round-figured birthday did bring with it a sense of having nothing to lose, a tendency to throw caution to the wind and think, 'Ah, what the hell: why not?'

And along with that sense came the realisation that I had probably held out long enough, and that Del couldn't really damage me at this point. I could afford to be more comfortable around him, and less bothered about how he might be affecting my prospects. That was a nice feeling: having reached 2020, Derek Trotter and I could most likely rub along together without me having to worry too much about it.

It also occurred to me that, after all these years of refusing to get involved, maybe it would be nice to pay back these convention-attending fans for that long-standing loyalty, while I still could.

What can I tell you? Reader, I weakened. Curiosity overcame me. A couple of my favourite charities were going to benefit, so that was also a clincher. I was persuaded to break the habit of a lifetime and go to the conference.

And I would have no cause to regret that I did, either.

By the way, let's just pause to reflect how oddly innocent those days – the days of late February 2020 – feel now. It was the dying embers of the age of normality, had we but known it – a time when people could happily gather and rub shoulders in a confined space in their hundreds (800 people, in fact, in four sittings across two days) without thinking anything much of it. Can you imagine such a time? It feels like ages ago now, doesn't it? Another lifetime, indeed, and a wonderfully carefree one – although, again, perhaps we didn't realise exactly how carefree. The only sign of the looming crisis in that Bedfordshire conference suite was a couple of hand-written notices requesting that we all kept our hands clean and some containers of antiseptic gel to help us do so.

In a mere matter of weeks, all the schools would be closed and the Prime Minister would be getting up behind a lectern on television every afternoon and saying all sorts of confusing and self-contradictory things about how we were meant to be behaving as a nation in order to contain this massive threat to our way of life and our economy. Yet at this point it was still possible to imagine that we might keep the whole thing at bay with a few strategically placed bottles of hand sanitiser.

A time of innocence indeed. A time before the fall. A time when someone of my distinguished years could happily volunteer to spend a weekend shaking hands and posing for photographs with 800 strangers without having to wonder too hard about whether it might kill him. Because it turned out (wouldn't you know it?) that I had agreed to do the biggest meet and greet event of my career on the eve of the biggest health crisis to afflict the world in the best part of a century. Were the gods trying to tell me something?

Would it have been prudent to do the event in full PPE, or a hazmat suit? Clearly, hindsight suggests that might not have been such a bad idea, although it might not have struck quite the right tone and it would certainly have spoiled the photographs. At the same time, wouldn't it have been ironic if the first time I managed to show up at an *Only Fools* fan convention, it managed to see me off once and for all? People would have been able to say: 'Ah, well. At least he died doing something he always said he never wanted to do.'

One thing was clear: after all these years of refusing to take part in this kind of thing, I was never just going to be able to cruise into that banqueting suite completely at ease. Setting aside the gathering clouds of a global pandemic, I found space to be anxious about the event in the build-up to it – really all the way to the door of the hotel and a little bit beyond.

Again it was those worries about letting people down that were prominent in my mind. Wasn't I bound to disappoint the conventioneers? I was so much younger when those programmes that they remember so well were made. I had more hair, and other things in my favour. Likely as not, that would be the image of me that was prominent in their thoughts – just as, in fact, it's the image of myself that's most prominent in mine, until I catch sight of myself in a mirror or while passing a shop window and am brutally reminded that a few years have gone by since then and won't be coming back.

All these people would be coming along expecting to see the bloke who did all that funny stuff in *Only Fools* and then this ageing primate walks in … Wouldn't they feel a bit deflated? Might they not even consider consulting the people at the Trades Descriptions office? All this was spinning around in my head as I pitched up with Gill and my daughter Sophie at the 'stage door' at the back of the hotel at 8.30 a.m. on the Saturday.

Still, Perry and the team of organisers who met me were very welcoming and reassuring. My job, I learned, would be to sit in an armchair at the centre of a very authentic mock-up of the Trotters' Peckham flat. Perry's collection of memorabilia had clearly been plundered to good effect in the construction of this set: the awful orange curtains, the stacks of cardboard boxes (RAJAH computers, made in Mauritius), the music centre with the Showaddywaddy and Bachelors LPs stacked nearby, the brown ceramic cheese caddy, the pineapple ice bucket, the gold-coloured hostess trolley, and the full-sized china Collie dog … all were present and correct. I had a little look around, felt like I was on familiar turf, at least, and then went 'backstage' to sit and wait until the doors opened and it was my time to appear.

As a performer, I'm normally fairly well in control of my nerves. But that morning, as more and more people kept coming back to check if I was OK and to ask me if there was anything I needed, and as each of those visitors brought news of the growing crowd of fans arriving outside, I began to feel nervous in a way that I realised I hadn't felt in years. Initially the only thing I requested from these enormously attentive chaperones was a cup of tea, but after a while, as the nerves continued to mount, I began to wonder whether I should have asked for a bottle of whisky, or possibly even a tranquilliser gun and a handful of pellets.

I remembered how Nick and I always used to be anxious on Sunday nights in the minutes before we went out in front of the audience to record the as-live portions of the show. We would both be pacing up and down and trying to shake off the worst of it, and wondering what mad streak in us made us put ourselves through this ordeal time and time again. It seemed to become a ritual as we passed each other at the back of the set: we would look at each other, like rabbits in headlights, and say, 'Why do we do this?' This felt like that all over again.

Eventually, though, it was time to be led down to the set and for the event to begin. When the door opened and I appeared there was a massive gale of applause and cheering from the assembled conventioneers, to the point where I was looking over my shoulder to see who else had come on behind me. This was a welcome worthy of Taylor Swift, surely. But no: it was all for me, which was very moving and certainly settled my trepidation. I seemed to have been forgiven for having got a little older since *Only Fools* was shot. Indeed, the fact that I had done so seemed to be cause for celebration. That was a relief. I took my place in the battered armchair in the Trotters' flat and the meeting and greeting started.

What a giant bowl of swirling emotions the following hours stirred up. I had thought I didn't need to go to a fan convention to know what the show meant to people. I felt I knew that already, from people coming up to me in the street and telling me. I knew it also from people writing to let me know. I knew how much people felt the characters in that show spoke to them and how certain episodes had had the power to lift people out of tough times by giving them something that made them laugh when they most needed it, and least expected it to be possible. I had more than once been asked to record a message in the voice of Del in the hope that, if played at the bedside, it might bring a loved one out of a coma. Now, that request will pull you up short, let me tell you. I had done as asked, too, and, on at least one occasion, had been assured that it had worked.

The lesson being: never underestimate the power of comedy or its value to people.

143

And then there were stories like the one I heard about Keith Drew. In 2016, Keith, who was from Frome, died at the age of seventy-six from acute myeloid leukaemia. In accordance with his wishes, his coffin arrived at Haycombe Crematorium in Bath in the back of a modified Reliant Regal – a Regal chopped and extended to become a bright yellow hearse, with Trotters Independent Trading written on the side of it. Paris, London, Peckham – and now Haycombe Crematorium, then.

The coffin was borne in to the strains of the show's theme song – a choice of ceremonial music which, I am led to believe, is made a fair amount: not quite enough to rival Robbie Williams singing 'Angels', maybe, but up there somewhere. I heard about the Drew family's plans in advance and felt I could only send them a letter of condolence in which I made a version of the remark I have found myself making so many times over the years: 'It is amazing that the show has meant so much to people.'

I also wrote, 'If the vicar is wearing a hat, tell him to keep an eye on it. I am sure your dad would appreciate that thought.'

I knew they would get the reference, and maybe you do, too. It's one of my favourite John Sullivan moments – Grandad's hat lobbed solemnly into his unfilled grave at the funeral by an ashen-faced Del and Rodney, except that it wasn't Grandad's hat, it was the vicar's. To build a moment of deep poignance, and then to softly undermine it in a way that's hugely funny but still leaves that poignancy intact, seems to me as good a mark as any of John's facility as a comedy writer. (Incidentally, if you want my own thoughts on what makes a good funeral, they are as follows: any one where you're in the congregation rather than on the front of the Order of Service. I suspect funerals are the one occasion when even an actor will decline the opportunity to be the main attraction.)

So, all in all, I reckoned I knew everything there was to know about the extent to which people had taken the show into their lives. John Sullivan's writing never shied away from the big things in life – birth, love, marriage, death and everything in between found its way into the drama, from the maternity ward to the graveside – and I knew that people associated the show with big moments in their own journeys.

But meeting all those fans face to face at the convention in that concerted way across a weekend took my appreciation of the relationship that people have with the show to another level completely. It was joyful, it was sobering; it made you proud, it made you humble. There was a lot of happiness, and many, many laughs. There were also many tattoos, which people were very happy to show me. One bloke had Del, Rodney and Grandad inked onto the length of his back. Another had a reproduction of the card game scene, with a smattering of other references to the show. These were done so well, with painstaking attention to detail – and what a commitment! I really didn't expect to have people hitching up their clothes in order to show me their torsos, arms and legs, but I was very grateful that they did. They were images to store alongside other pictorial tributes to the show that I have encountered on trucks, vans and even on a narrowboat. Amazing, really. There was a lovely sentence I kept hearing from people, again and again: 'Thank you from the bottom of my heart.' And quite apart from anything else, it goes without saying that, when people are thanking you, you're always glad that it's from the bottom of their hearts, rather than from the heart of their bottoms.

But there was also some sadness. Some people who came and sat down beside me were in tears and could hardly get the words out that they wanted to say. I thought about that a lot afterwards.

They could have been in tears for all sorts of reasons, of course: the sheer overwhelming nature of my animal magnetism, for example, could easily have reduced them to that state, much as millions of people before them have been rendered emotional down the years by my long succession of gilded performances on stage and screen. It would have been entirely reasonable – indeed, to be expected. 'Jason-mania', the press have tended to call it. The Beatles, I am assured – including my age-sake Ringo – had much the same effect on people, albeit in slightly more limited circumstances.

Some people, though, told me stories about how *Only Fools* had helped them out in a bad moment – how laughing at it had eased them through a difficult patch in their lives, which it choked them up to recount. It choked me up, too, to hear them talk about it. Some people told me that they had been in a very dark place and that they felt the show had dragged them back from the edge. On more than one occasion, I sat and listened to someone thank me for, in effect, saving their life. Which is something to hear in a conference suite in Bedfordshire on a Saturday afternoon. It wasn't me, of course: it was the character, the writing, the cast and everything that had gone into the creation of the show, but it was still staggering to be made so graphically and intimately aware of the profound impact that the show had had.

But there were other times when the tears seemed to flow for no specific reason that the person told me about, and in those cases I think I understood what was going on. It was like those moments when football teams win something and the television camera pans to the crowd and picks out supporters who are in tears. And initially you think, 'Oh, come on – get a grip on your knickers. It's only football, for heaven's sake.'

And then you think a bit harder about it and realise that they're not really weeping about the trophy or the match or the result; they're weeping about the people they know who would have enjoyed sharing that particular moment with

147

them but who aren't there, for whatever reason. It's a moment of commemoration, really. I think a lot of that was going on with the people who sat down beside me and suddenly found they were crying. They weren't crying about me, or the show, or for themselves; they were crying about the people they shared the show with and who had loved it as much as they did. Crying for past times.

I can entirely relate to that. There are plenty of friends of mine from the show who are no longer with us: Lennard Pearce, Roger Lloyd-Pack, Buster Merryfield, Ken Mac-Donald who died far too young at fifty, and John Sullivan, the show's creator, who was also lost to us prematurely at sixty-four, when he clearly had so much more writing left in him. I think of them when I think of the show, and it stirs deep feelings and memories in me, too.

I think those feelings are another reason why I have been careful about engaging with the show since it ended and why I have largely fought shy of doing so. I've been protecting myself. But I'm glad I let my guard drop this once and allowed myself to share it. For those few hours, I was like any other fan of *Only Fools*: keen to celebrate the show and keen to keep it alive in any way that I could.

I made a lot of new friends over those two days – and also reacquainted myself with some old ones. John Challis, who played Boycie, was there, and so was Sue Holderness, who played Marlene. So was John Lyons, who played Toolan in *A Touch of Frost*, and Tim Healy, who is Gastric in *Still Open*

All Hours. It was great to see them all and to grab a slice of pizza with them at lunchtime. (One slice of pizza each, I should say. We weren't sharing the same slice.)

And then, at one point on the first day of the convention, another familiar figure suddenly plonked himself down on the chair beside me, smiled broadly and reached for my hand. Blimey, I thought: this bloke's a dead ringer for Ricky Hatton, the boxer.

It was Ricky Hatton, the boxer.

Huge fan of the show, Ricky. Mind you, he could be a fan of whatever show he liked and I, personally, wouldn't pick a fight with him over it. He would later leave the venue proudly clutching a replica of the front end of a Trotters' van. I was happy to sign it for him. I thought about reversing the tables and asking him if I could put: 'To Ricky. It was a good fight, but in the end, I think you'll agree, I had just a little bit too much for you to cope with. All the best with the recovery, and have your people contact mine about the possibility of a rematch, although bear in mind that my schedule is very busy – David Jason.' But I thought better of it, and there probably wouldn't have been room, even on the whole front end of a Trotters' van.

To be perfectly frank, I'm not sure what Ricky wanted with a bit of a Reliant Regal, because my understanding is that he possesses a fully functioning whole one somewhere. He bought it for a modest sum in 2009 and once filmed a very funny skit of himself leaving the gym to go home after a hard day's workout, and appearing to get into an extremely swish, two-tone Rolls-Royce (complete with personalised number plate), only to swing out from behind it in the Reliant and nip off across the car park.

Anyway, Ricky was happy to be part of the crowd that day, a fan like any other.

Just another person, in other words, wandering around a hotel conference suite in Bedfordshire with a signed car part. What's so unusual about that?

CHAPTER SEVEN

On first impressions and lasting memories in Only Fools and Horses

As I sat on that replica set, amid those old, familiar props at the *Only Fools and Horses* 2020 convention, so many memories came flooding back.

I was reminded of reading the script for what turned out to be the very first episode of the show, where the description of the setting for the opening scene, in a flat in a tower block in Peckham, was very specific.

> Nothing is permanent. The settee and two armchairs are from three separate suites as the other pieces were used as make-weights in various swaps. There are three TV sets, one colour, one black and white, and one with its back off awaiting repair ... The décor is clean but gaudy. Dozens of clashing patterns. It should look like the start of a bad trip.

Well, the organisers of the convention had certainly got that last bit right.

And thinking about that script I was sent spinning back in my memory to a lift in the BBC's Television Rehearsal Rooms in glamorous Acton in west London, circa 1980, a sixties building on the Victoria Road lovingly known to one and all as the Acton Hilton.

You are to imagine me, at this point in my career, as a forty-year-old actor with something of a reputation for secondary roles in television programmes, who longs to find a show that he can front. I have tried out in a handful of things, with varying degrees of promise, but each of which has ended up bringing to mind nothing so much as the words 'damp' and 'squib'.

Indeed, I am a forty-year-old actor about whom a reviewer in *The Stage* newspaper has recently said: 'Somewhere there is a writer whose ideas Mr Jason can execute to great effect, but they have not yet met.'

I am a forty-year-old actor who would very much like to put that right, and who is battling on cheerfully to that end, but who is starting to have a few nagging worries that he might be running out of options and time.

Meanwhile I am taking a break from rehearsing for *Open All Hours* and heading down to the canteen for lunch – which, knowing the standard of the catering at the Acton Hilton, will likely be a gourmet affair, and will almost certainly be featuring a handful of Wall's finest sausages, baked to within an inch of their lives, and accompanied by a stodgy dollop of cauliflower cheese which has been kept alive, possibly very much against its will, for a number of weeks under a heating lamp.

Delicious, actually. Don't knock it. I'm getting hungry thinking about it even now. Ronnie Barker always used to say, as we adjourned for meals at such moments, 'You can't be funny on an empty stomach.' He was absolutely right, and when I was working with Ronnie we broke religiously for lunch in order to make sure we were never accused of trying to be.

Anyway, accompanying me in the lift that day is not Ronnie Barker but Syd Lotterby, the producer of *Open All Hours*, who presses a large-ish manila envelope on me and asks, in a very casual way, if I'd be prepared to have a look at its contents and see what I think. I take the envelope away, open it up that evening at home in my flat, while seated, no doubt, at the brilliantly devised kitchen 'table' mentioned earlier, and I pull out the script for episode one of something called *Readies* by John Sullivan.

At that point in my career, had I opened the envelope and pulled out some actual readies, it would not have gone amiss. I might even have been able to afford a better table. But you take what you're given.

I start reading, and straight away I get a good feeling about what I'm seeing. The hurling of insults between characters is, of course, a sitcom staple, but the insults between these particular characters seem to have a different class of cut and thrust about them. I start to feel that certain twitch that you get when you first read a punchy script and realise that you would get a lot of fun out of delivering its lines.

I am particularly drawn to the exchange that the character called Del has with his much younger brother, Rodney, in which Del says: 'For the first three months of the pregnancy, you were treated as an ulcer. And to this day I sometimes think the original diagnosis was correct.' I can imagine doing a good job on that line.

And, of course, somewhere in the middle of all this, there is the definitive statement of Derek Trotter's 'art of the deal', which is at least as astute as anything that Donald Trump has ever managed to come up with in that line: 'Everything between you and I, split straight down the middle – 60:40.' I can imagine having a lot of joy with a line like that, too.

But it's not just the quality of the individual lines. I'm straight away feeling I know who these characters are, and instantly seeing how that interplay between the three generations – young, middle-aged, elderly – rings true and works. That sense of immediate familiarity, and the warmth that follows from it, is by no means a common thing in a pilot script. Indeed, it's pretty much the holy grail in that area for the obvious reason that it's not an easy thing to pull off. It takes a writer with skill to manage it and when you come across it as a hopeful actor, sitting in your flat one evening, it's a pretty exciting thing. I imagine metal detectorists feel a similar sensation when they sink the trowel in and catch a glimpse of something golden.

All that said, did I think I was holding the potential for two decades-worth of lucrative work and the material for a piece of television that would one day smash all records for comedy audience figures and leave me, in 2020, signing car parts in a hotel convention and banqueting suite in Bedfordshire?

Of course not. For one thing, I was well aware by this point in my career that an awful lot happens before the script you're excitedly reading becomes a show on a screen. It's got to be cast, rehearsed, directed, lit, shot, edited ... Many's the slip t'wixt cup and lip, they say, and they're not wrong. The show you eventually sit down to watch can land up a million miles from the one you enthusiastically envisaged as you first turned the pages with images of glory and long nights at the Bafta Awards ceremony chasing through your mind.

My path into the dusky wood of showbusiness up to this point was already strewn with examples (rather too many, to be perfectly honest) of shows that all too painfully demonstrated the gap between hope and experience in this area – and we'll have cause to consider some of those in due course.

For now, suffice it to say that I had read a lot of pilot scripts for comedies, and I knew enough to know that this one called *Readies* was strong, and that there was potential in it, if it was done right. But anything more than that, I knew better than to have a firm opinion about.

The next day I gave the envelope back to Syd, saying I thought the script obviously had something going for it, and that if it ever reached that stage, I would love to have a stab at playing the character in it called Derek Trotter. I seem to remember Syd looking a bit deflated by that. I think he'd had me in mind for the role of Grandad and maybe saw me doing it as some sort of variant on my role as Blanco in *Porridge*, with me dressing up to play old. I really don't think he expected me to latch on to Del, someone who was meant to be in his early thirties. There would have to be some delicate conversations between a few people before that could happen.

So that was my first encounter with the Trotters. The British public's first encounter with that family was technically in the trailer for the opening episode, which eventually went out on BBC1 in the autumn of 1981. By then, of course, the show had ceased to be *Readies* and had gained a new title, clipped from the saying 'only fools and horses work', which John tried to pass off to some anxious executives at the BBC as an authentic London expression, although actually it had its origins in American vaudeville. Close enough.

There was, inevitably, a lot of discussion about the wisdom or otherwise of John's desire to remove the word 'work' from that expression, and about what you were left with when you did so. The BBC were convinced it was going to be puzzling for people. They weren't wrong. One day a quick poll was taken randomly in the BBC bar to see what people thought the title meant. Somebody thought it was a quotation from Shakespeare and somebody else thought it was the title of Lester Piggott's life story. You will still find people for whom the title is a bit of a mystery even today.

But that was the point, of course. It wasn't really about whether or not it immediately made sense, it was about whether people would notice and remember it. The oddness of the title, and the slight puzzle of it, were exactly the ingredients that would make it stick.

Well, that was the plan, anyway. But it's interesting to watch that first promo now. It feels like an artefact from another age – to an extent to which the show itself, I would say, does not. (The fact that *Only Fools* is still being repeated on a practically constant rotation would seem to bear me out in that point of view.)

In the promo, the BBC voice-over alerts us to 'a new comedy series starring David Jason and Nicholas Lyndhurst as brotherly business partners'. There's an establishing shot of Del and Rodney loading boxes into the back of the Reliant Regal, and then there are two sequences from the show, very basically knocked together. The first of them has Del and Rodney, back in that chaotically furnished flat now, arguing about the merits of having traded a selection of unwanted items, secured at auction, for a batch of one-legged turkeys.

Del defensively protests at the description of the turkeys as 'one-legged', preferring the term 'damaged'.

'How many legs did they have?' counters Rodney, unsympathetically.

Del briefly wears the expression of a cornered man.

'I'm in no mood for trick questions,' he eventually replies.

We then, with just a little burst of music to mark the transition, cut to a table at the Nag's Head and witness part of a conversation between Del, Rodney and Roger Lloyd-Pack as Trigger, where Del is wielding a calculator and the three of them are squabbling over some sums.

'But he's got GCEs in Maths and Art,' says Trigger, in defence of Rodney.

'So what does that prove?' Del replies. 'He can paint by numbers.'

Cue the BBC voice-over guy: 'Tomorrow at 8.30 on BBC1,' he fruitily confirms.

And that's it. How primitive this little scrap of promo feels by comparison with today's great works of advertising. There is no jump-cutting, no fast and furious flipping through the length of the programme and certainly no attempt to give a flavour of the whole thing in condensed form, which is what you might get now. There is no hulla-balloo – indeed, nobody seems to be banging a drum in any way at all. The viewer is modestly offered two small lumps of the show and left to draw his or her own conclusion about whether the rest looks worth tuning in for or not.

Quaint and understated as that trailer seems – almost, I would say, to the point of being ineffectual – I rather warm to it. Trailers in the modern style are a big bugbear of mine. These days the instinct seems to be to give absolutely every-thing away about a new show and to leave nothing to chance or the viewer's imagination. That's annoying in the case of a drama, but it's absolute death for comedy. You'll spend ages working on the build-up to a gag or to a big visual reveal, trying to get the weight and the timing right so that it has maximum impact when it happens – and then the trailer for the show will jump straight in and expose the critical moment out of context.

I've had endless arguments with people in broadcasting about this tendency down the years. I had them over *A Touch of Frost* where I sometimes felt too much of the story we had patiently worked to unfold in the show was being disclosed in advance. And I have been having them again more recently with regard to some of the trails for *Still Open All Hours*, where the temptation to explode a punchline still seems to be felt.

159

My line would always be, 'Why are you showing the end product? If it were a custard pie sequence, would you be showing the person that gets hit?'

The response is usually, 'It's a hook. It will get people to watch.'

'Maybe,' I say, 'but now you've ruined the joke.'

I haven't quite managed to work out who is chiefly at fault in this desire to screen the whole show in bits in the trailer. I can't believe the British public has lost the patience to wait for a story to unfold, or ceased to enjoy a bit of anticipation. ITV does it in order to sell adverts, but what's the BBC's excuse?

But I realise I am wasting my sweetness on the desert air, as Lawrence of Arabia always used to say while his camel nodded silently in sympathy. Broadcasting is a ferociously competitive business now, the fight for audience share is brutal, and nobody wants to leave anything to chance by not shouting about their wares loudly enough. It's not about holding back any more, it's about showing them exactly what you've got – and as much of it as possible, in as short a space of time as possible. Most trailers these days feel more like a mugging than an invitation to view, and I'm not sure the shows really benefit from it.

I often think with a shudder how different things might have been for *Only Fools* if we hadn't had the power to put our feet down and control the images that went out in advance. Consider the Batman and Robin sequence, from the 'Heroes and Villains' Christmas special episode in 1996. By that point in its history, the show was big enough that we were fighting a battle on two fronts – with the BBC publicity department, who wanted to get out ahead of the broadcast to attract viewers, and with the press, who now covered *Only Fools* location shoots as if they were breaking news stories and who were determined to get exclusive pictures of future scenes from the show.

Of course, that growing attention, from public and press alike, was one of the reasons the show stopped filming on location in London and moved elsewhere – to Bristol, substantially, but also to Ipswich, Salisbury, Brighton, Hull … You would possibly be surprised how many towns in the UK have boasted a Peckham street market at some time or other and how easy it is to convert somewhere to a convincing approximation of London by the simple means of putting a red bus or a black cab somewhere in the background. Cost, it can't be denied, was another factor in that relocation, because London became a very pricey place to film things as the 1980s turned into the 1990s. But mostly we were simply crowded out of the capital by our own popularity.

I can remember the early days of filming regularly in Chapel Market in Islington, which was very convenient for me, living a couple of miles away, off Oxford Street. But I also remember that location getting gradually more inconvenient in every other respect. As the show's reputation grew, so the groups of interested onlookers would gather in ever increasing numbers until getting the quiet you needed for a take became almost impossible. During the school lunch hour, we would get swarmed all over by kids from the nearby secondary school, and at 3.45, when the bell went for the end of the school day, we would have to knock it on the head entirely because we knew there would be no peace in the near future.

Nick Lyndhurst had the best story from that time. We were filming in Chapel Market in the tipping rain one day and had taken a break under umbrellas to wait for a gap in the weather so we could resume. Nick suddenly found himself joined under his umbrella by a small girl who appeared out of nowhere. This girl fixed Nick with the steely, inquisitive look that only the very young can muster.

'What are you doing?' she wanted to know.

Nick explained that we were making a television programme.

'What's it called?' she said.

'*Only Fools and Horses*,' said Nick.

The girl cast a long look around the rain-drenched scene and then brought her eyes back to Nick.

'Well, where are the horses, then?'

Fools, yes: she could see those all right. But no horses. Kids don't miss a trick.

Anyway, when the Batman and Robin sequence was filmed, we were well into the show's Bristol phase. That famous costumed appearance was very patiently set up in the writing. You knew Del and Rodney were on their way to a fancy-dress party (or what they thought was a fancy-dress party), but you had no idea what they were dressed as. You've only been hearing their conversation in the van in voice-over, so when the van eventually breaks down, and one of them says, 'I'm not getting out dressed like this,' you are still none the wiser.

And that sets up the great suspense-film shot, with the camera at ground level, of the car door opening and the ridiculous pixie boot emerging and setting itself down on the ground. Then you cut to the front of the car, where Del Boy comes round and is revealed, finally, as Batman, prior to Rodney joining him and being revealed, finally, as Robin.

Beyond this, of course, lies the extra joke that they are not, as they believe, on their way to a fancy-dress party, but are actually bound for a wake, the host of the party having died, unbeknown to them, in the intervening days. Anyway, as far as we were concerned, even a glimpse of Del or Rodney in those stupid costumes before the episode was broadcast – indeed at any moment before that foot in the boot was seen to hit the ground – would have been ruinous. You might just as well have shredded all that careful build-up, done away with the emerging-from-the-car sequence, and simply shown Del and Rodney at home putting on the costumes. That sequence was all about the delayed revelation. That was the whole joy of it.

Hence the decision to shoot the scene after midnight, when the minimal number of people would be around to witness it. Not only was the area of Bristol where we were working boarded off, with security people posted around the perimeter, but we had some bright spotlights put up around the action and shining away from it, so anybody trying to take a picture would get dazzled and be unable to pick much out.

Furthermore, once it was in the can, we had the clout to tell the BBC that nothing showing Del and Rodney in those outfits should be leaked. That way we managed to hold it all back until the night of broadcast. A picture in the paper could have spoiled it. A trailer would have killed it stone dead.

The lesson being: in comedy as in life, keep your powder dry with all your might.

There were so many times on *Only Fools* when we were laughing so hard that we could barely get the scene shot, and, despite all the anxiety about exposure, one of those was that freezing cold night in Bristol. Just the sight of each other in those costumes kept causing Nick and I to go in turns. We needed so many retakes that it was threatening to get light before we were wrapped.

Another was the scene from series three where Grandad shows Rodney and Del the silver cigarette lighter that his own grandfather had carried with him, allegedly, during the

Boer War. Grandad explains that a bullet from a sniper would have struck his grandfather in the heart if it hadn't been for the protection of this piece of silver in his tunic. Rodney is obviously moved and impressed by this influential, life-saving relic.

'Jeez, it saved his life,' he says.

'Not really,' says Grandad. 'See, the bullet ricocheted up his nose and blew his brains out.'

Now, that line just set us all going. We could not get the scene down for corpsing. Take after take ensued – to the point where Ray Butt, the producer, who had a shooting schedule to stick to, was getting seriously annoyed with us. I had to say to him, 'If you think this is easy, come down here and have a go at it yourself.'

And then there was the scene with the urn of ashes and the street-cleaning lorry. Del and Rodney have been charged with the care of Trigger's grandfather's mortal remains and have rested them briefly on the edge of the pavement, only for a street-cleaning lorry to come along and suck them up. There then ensues a panicked conversation with the driver in his cab.

'You've just sucked up our urn,' Rodney and I urgently inform him.

'Oh my God. What was he – a little kitten?' replies the horrified driver.

In that case, it was the cameraman, up in the cab and shooting out of the window, who couldn't control himself.

He would get the shakes and then Nick and I would go in response to him, and once again the circle of mirth would be complete and the take would go to waste. We had to haul out the cameraman and replace him for that shot in the end. If we hadn't, I seriously think we would still be there by the side of that road even now.

But then there were the sequences at the opposite end from those moments of hilarity: the poignant moments in John Sullivan's writing that not only brought tears to the eyes of the viewers, but also to those of us doing the acting, as well. So many of those come to mind: the shot, for instance, where Del holds the figurine off the top of the wedding cake at Rodney and Cassandra's wedding and is clearly wondering what might have been if he hadn't sacrificed so much of his own life to look after the rest of his family. Such a touching moment, that – another of those points where the comedy opens up to reveal its human depths.

Another one was the scene, following the death in real life of Buster Merryfield, where Del and Rodney scattered Uncle Albert's ashes on the sea, after the visit to the French village where he spent the war (and where a surprising number of people seemed to be going around the place who were bald with big white beards, as Albert was).

Or, perhaps most emphatically, there was that moment where Del and Rodney, having just become millionaires thanks to the sale of the surprisingly rare watch, go back to the Nag's Head to tell everyone about their new-found fortune. There's a pause while everyone in the pub digests the news – a pause shared with the viewers at home, I think, who are also at this moment realising that this is the point where everything is changed and that nothing can really be the same after this. These two no-hopers who have always told themselves they'll be millionaires finally are millionaires and the story is complete, in a way. And then, slowly, among the punters in the Nag's Head, a round of applause starts up. And it grows and what it starts to feel like is a round of applause for the show itself, which has taken us on this extraordinary narrative voyage through to its completion. It was incredibly moving to watch, and even more moving to be a part of.

Should we have left it there? With hindsight, it would have been the perfect get-out point, the neatest of tie-ups. But hindsight is easy. There was so much pressure to keep going – pressure on John, pressure on the cast, pressure on the producers. Extraordinary numbers of people loved the show and wanted more of it, in the form of specials each year. People *still* want more of the show, even now, all these years later, when John Sullivan isn't even around to supply it. It's still the first question I get asked: 'Do you think there could be any more?' And I always have to say, 'Well, no – not for as long as John is no longer with us, and all the indications are that that situation is set to continue.'

I understand the point people make about not overdoing things and leaving the audience wanting more, and about getting out at exactly the right time. The model in this area that people always hold up is John Cleese and Connie Booth who did two near-perfect series of *Fawlty Towers* and then called it quits. There is a lot to be said for that, clearly. At the same time, if we had stopped *Only Fools* after two series, people would never have seen the best of it. And when it came to it, we were ending something with which people had built up a relationship over twenty years. Many of our viewers could barely remember a time when the show hadn't been around and had grown up with and alongside the characters. We felt a responsibility to them. It was hard to find the best moment and the perfect way. Maybe we did go back to the well a couple more times than we should have done – and maybe being rich, as they were, briefly, in 2001, didn't suit the Trotters as well as being poor. Nevertheless, there were some really good things in those later Christmas specials. I would have hated to have missed those.

Mostly when I think about *Only Fools* these days, I think about what a great group of people was assembled for that show and how we all blended together so well, not just in front of the cameras but also off it, which is so important. There was a really solid team ethic, which you are definitely going to need if a show is going to be successful in the long run. I used to love going into the Acton Hilton for the

Monday morning read-throughs. The latest script would have been posted to you at home and you would have had a look at it there, and maybe made a few notes. And then you would come in at the start of the week, meet any cast members who might be new to that episode, fall on the tea and biscuits and then sit round a table and read through the script aloud.

That was always a great session, very relaxed, full of laughter, where you could feel the episode beginning to come to life. People would always read things in a way that you hadn't thought of when you had read it in your head – ways that squeezed something else out of a line.

After the read-through, we'd move on to the physical rehearsals, blocking out the set-ups that we were going to take out on location and perform in the studio in front of the live audience at the end of the week. That was where the work started to get more serious, but I loved that part of the process probably most of all, looking for opportunities to add gestures and bits of business, constantly asking yourself, 'What's the best way to play this? Is there anything more here? Are we getting the absolute maximum out of this set-up?'

A lot of the work in those early days was editing. Situation comedies were thirty minutes long: that was the law. Nobody really queried why it was the law. It simply was. But John naturally tended to write long. No matter what the brief was, he would come in over-length. Like the time, for instance, when he had to come up with a quick three-minute skit that we could use at the Royal Variety Show. The first version John delivered was more like twenty-five minutes. That was just the way John seemed to operate. So, every week we were throwing out masses of material in order to bring the show in on time. And a lot of that material was really good. So, after endless appeals to the BBC, the programme was allotted a fifty-minute slot. At which point John, of course, began writing scripts that came in at an hour and still had to be trimmed.

Still, longer was better, in this case – definitely. Again, it set the show apart from other comedies and was another indication that what you were looking at with *Only Fools* was a comedy drama that couldn't be contained within the conventional sitcom timeframe. At the same time, that expanded length was a rod for our own backs. Trying to get a fifty-minute show done in a week, instead of a thirty-minute show, merely meant that initially all of us were working our socks off, six days a week. By the time we got round to filming the studio portion of the show on a Sunday night, we were dead on our (sockless) feet.

When we got settled into it, though, the shoots got spaced out and we would have ten days for each episode, which was much more do-able. And all of the effort was worth it. That first series of fifty-minute episodes contained some of the show's strongest material and averaged audiences above

16 million – tremendous figures for a regular week night outside the Christmas season.

Of course, it wasn't all sweat and labour with our mighty pickaxes at the dramatic coalface. During periods of down-time, and at least once a week if possible, I used to organise paper plane-building contests for the cast. We would all have to construct a plane and then fly them out of the window of the Acton Hilton to see whose could travel furthest.

I pride myself on my paper plane construction and my ability to send a sheet of A4 further than it has any business going, but I have to concede that Nick Lyndhurst was dev-ilishly good at it, a master paper plane builder who would create these origami monsters that floated practically half way across Acton.

Great times, then, with great people. So it's sobering for me to reflect that I might not even have been cast and might never have known any of it – not a single minute. Again, one reflects on the thinness of the thread that binds all these things together.

Nick Lyndhurst was the first person to be given a role in *Only Fools*. John Howard Davies, the BBC's head of comedy, seems to have had him in mind from the get-go. Nick had been one of the sons in *Butterflies*, the Wendy Craig and Geoffrey Palmer comedy, but perhaps more rel-evantly he had also played opposite Ronnie Barker in the *Porridge* spin-off, *Going Straight*. In that series, where

Fletcher gets out of prison and returns to his life in north London, Nick played Fletcher's son, Raymond, who appeared to have an A-level in lethargy and a stooped look that made his gangly arms appear to be a bit too long for his body. There's a very clear connection between Raymond and Rodney.

They settled on Lennard Pearce for Grandad very quickly, too, whatever notions Syd might have had about pushing me for the role. Lennard came on the recommendation of a trusted agent and, as with Nick, I don't think anyone else was auditioned for that part.

Del, though, was a touch more problematic. Enn Reitel, a great comic actor and a brilliant voice specialist, was apparently the first port of call. But it turned out he was already busy on something. Jim Broadbent was offered the role but turned it down because he was about to start work in a play. I'm told that Robin Nedwell, who was famous for appearing in the *Doctor in the House* comedy series, and Billy Murray, who was later on *The Bill* and *EastEnders*, may also have been considered and either set themselves aside or were set aside for various reasons.

There may well have been others. Why, perhaps you, dear reader, were considered for the role, too, and turned it down. It would hardly come as a shock to me. By the most conservative estimate, I was merely the fifth option on the list headed 'People the BBC would be interested in talking to about playing Derek Trotter.'

Which I suppose I could have been offended by, had I chosen to be. Some actors, I'm sure, would have been terribly sniffy about not having been offered something first, let alone about being offered something fifth. People of a certain actorly stature would no doubt have seen themselves as far too grand for such hand-me-downs.

But I was forty and I think a bit of maturity played into my hands here. I knew there were all sorts of reasons why people got approached for roles. It was up to me whether I took them personally or not. The fact was, eventually I was offered the chance to go and read for the part, and at that point it really didn't matter how many other people had been through the door before me. My attitude was: I understand all the reasons why you didn't come to me first. But I'm now going to show you why you should have done.

The lesson being: you don't need to be the first in line. Just be the best you can be when you get to the front of the queue.

Being tall, both Enn Reitel and Jim Broadbent would both, on the face of it, have made a much more plausible brother for Nick Lyndhurst. But, of course, it was much better that Del and Rodney *didn't* resemble each other. I remember, in the earliest proper meeting that I had about the show, when I was asked to go in and read with Nick, saying, in order to keep myself in the running for the job as much as anything else: 'One of them could be the milkman's.' And, of course, there was that wonderful insinuation through-out the show that Rodney and Del might not share a genetic father – that notion, never over-played but con-stantly hovering in the background, that only the two of them really believe they are brothers, while everybody else has their doubts.

It mattered that Del was smaller than Rodney for the physical nature of their relationship, too. The smaller man punching up is always funnier, or certainly less problematic, than the bigger man punching down. Without that dispar-ity in height between the two, some of Del's bossing around of Rodney could have looked a bit like bullying. Interest-ingly, John Sullivan's sister, Maureen, was thirteen years older than him, so he was well placed to explore that kind of sibling relationship which is brotherly but also very strongly parental. That was true for Del's relationship with Rodney, and it can be no coincidence that John stipulated a thirteen-year gap between those two as well.

It took a while, though, to persuade John that I was the right person to play Del – entirely because he had never seen me do anything like it. Syd Lotterby, Ray Butt and I had worked on the pilot for a show entitled *It's Only Me – Whoever I Am*, written by Roy Clarke, who was the man behind *Open All Hours*. The lead character was loosely based on Granville and was a chap from Rochdale called Quentin who lived very much in the clutches of his mother, who was played by the excellent and very funny Patricia Hayes.

Alas, that show turned out to be another item on the list of disappointments that I mentioned earlier. Such a let-down. Roy Clarke is a tremendous writer and I really thought the show was a strong proposition. It had that crucial ingredient for a sitcom – a central character thwarted by his predicament, who longs to escape. And it was a situation that people could relate to and find funny and poignant.

Adding to the excitement, the pilot was commissioned to be shown as a one-off in the *Comedy Playhouse* strand in 1974, and that was bound to raise your hopes. The BBC in those days used *Comedy Playhouse* as a testing ground for new comedies. Other programmes that began as single comedies in that slot and then graduated to become their own series included *Steptoe and Son*, *Till Death Us Do Part*, *Up Pompeii*, *The Liver Birds*, *Are You Being Served?*, *Last of the Summer Wine* ... do I need to go on? Basically, great swathes of the history of BBC sitcoms had rocketed to success off the launchpad of *Comedy Playhouse*. I was really convinced that *It's Only Me* would follow them into the sky, too, and finally prove to the BBC and the watching nation that I was someone who could carry a television series as a leading player.

I was wrong. The single show went out, as planned, and people drew the conclusion that one episode was quite enough, thank you. Chalk it up as another in my long series of failed attempts to find a comedy vehicle that I could sit behind the wheel of. (I still don't think my hunch about the show was an altogether wild one. Indeed, you could say it was entirely supported a few years later when Ronnie Corbett had some success with a sitcom called *Sorry!*, the premise of which – thwarted man unable to slip out past domineering mother – was very similar. But hey. You win some, you lose some.)

The fact was, the roles I was getting tended to have the word 'hapless' appended to them. I could see the justice of that description – certainly once I'd looked the word up. It was a polite way of suggesting that I played losers, basically – people for whom existence was a long series of let-downs on various scales. People for whom the crisp bowl at life's great party was forever getting dampened.

And now here was Del – this bright, sharp, noisy chancer who bounced forward off the balls of his feet rather than dragging his heels. Del was someone who lost out all the time, too, but you wouldn't have known it, and that was the delightful and engaging aspect of his character. His energy was the energy of a born winner: he just happened to be a born winner who never won.

Typically, Granville in *Open All Hours* would be found resting his chin on his hand which flattened his mouth and pushed his cheek up, making him look weary with the cards that life had dealt him. Del, on the other hand, rarely had a lugubrious moment that lasted longer than it took the next big scheme to form in his mind. He was going to play his hand, whatever feeble cards fate had put in it. More than that, he was going to sneak a look at the other players' hands if he felt that a little light cheating might advance his chances.

Yet he was also a highly moral and warmly human figure in many important ways, even while being completely dodgy at other moments. He was a wonderful, rounded mess, which was what made him so lifelike and ultimately so appealing. He could flog you your own fountain pen to make a few quid, but he would give away his last penny to someone in need. And there was something rather wonderfully puppyish about him. He kept coming back for more. Life would insist on pushing him down, but he would be like a beach ball under water: you press down on it but it slips out to the side of your hands and flips back up.

So, John had his doubts about whether my face fitted, and I could see why he did so. This part was completely different from any of the roles that I had been playing. But that, equally, was why I became so keen to land the job. I was out to show that there was more to me than characters whose scenes ended on a sigh. Del's confidence, the fact that he had all the chat, and more front than Blackpool in August, meant he was nothing like me personally. But that only drew me to him even more strongly. I imagined it would feel wonderful to wrap yourself in all those layers of confidence, if only for a while. But in order to find out, I had to prove myself first.

I read twice for the show: first with Nick, and the second time, after a call-back, a few days later, with Nick and Lennard. And that second reading clinched it. The three of us simply clicked. It was obvious to everyone in the room, including John. There was no 'give us a couple of days to think about it and we'll let you know'. I was handed the job at the end of the reading and the three of us went off to the BBC bar to celebrate this new show we were going to be in – where, incidentally, none of us were staff members, so we couldn't buy an alcoholic drink to wet the baby's head properly, and had to settle for tea.

It's so interesting to me how success can alter people's perception of the history of things. Because *Only Fools* is now perceived to have been a success, people assume it was *always* a success – that glory was the only thing it knew. I sometimes get the feeling that people have that perception about my career, too: that people look at the level you eventually reached and forget about the struggles and setbacks you might have experienced along the way. I hope that if these pages are making anything clear, it's that there were certainly struggles and setbacks in my case.

The same was true of *Only Fools*. Far from being rapturously received by an eager British public from the get-go, it struggled to get out onto the runway and almost came a cropper before it was even airborne. John Sullivan was interested in writing about contemporary working-class people who had a bit of money to splash around and were quite flash with it. It was something, John felt, that nobody had really brought to the screen before – an area unexplored in television comedy writing.

And then, before *Only Fools* could get off the ground, *Minder* came along on ITV, with Dennis Waterman and John Thaw, focusing on a very similar vein in modern London life, albeit west London rather than south London, and for a different kind of dramatic purpose. But John was gutted when that happened because he thought he had been beaten to the punch and it wasn't clear what the attitude of the BBC was going to be to the arrival of this highly successful rival on the main competing channel.

But these things can cut both ways: sometimes another production in the same area steals your thunder; another time it simply suggests that your hunch was right, that there is interest out there, that the time is right. In this case, the BBC decided to follow suit. As it happened, *Minder* could be said to have blazed the trail, but it could just as easily have cut *Only Fools* off altogether.

Even when it made it into production, our show was twice on the verge of being cancelled: after series one and after series two. It didn't open to a fanfare and in a blaze of glory. Frankly, there was nobody in the cast who could have ensured that it did. You have to remember that none of us were actors that people would tune in to watch just to see what we were up to. I had a certain profile, on account of *Open All Hours*, and Nick did, on account of *Butterflies*, but neither of us was a big enough star to 'open' a show, as they say. And probably on account of that – in a Catch-22 kind of situation – the BBC didn't seem to feel particularly inclined to throw the weight of their publicity machine behind the series. *Only Fools* crept onto the screen very quietly.

Viewing figures for that first series didn't rise above the 7 million mark, which was an undistinguished audience in those days when there were only (can you believe it?) three channels to choose between. By contrast, *Open All Hours* would be getting 14 to 15 million viewers around this time.

It's interesting now to look back at the BBC Broadcasting Research Viewing Panel report on the first series of *Only Fools*. In order to gauge how well a show had gone down, and to get more detail than viewing figures alone would provide, the BBC would send questionnaires out for sets of viewers to complete and then compile a report from their responses. I think it's fair to say that writers and actors tended to be sceptical about this stuff, but the suits at the BBC seemed to set a great store by it, and clearly the destiny of shows could rise and fall on the basis of it.

The report compiled after the first series of *Only Fools* indicated that most people found it 'entertaining, amusing and well written on the whole'. So that was good. Nevertheless, there was apparently 'a fairly general feeling that it had got off to a slow start'. To the question, 'Would you welcome a second series?', 41 per cent of respondents replied, 'Yes, very much.' Again, not bad, but at the same time, not exactly an overwhelming gale of enthusiasm. Thirty-five per cent said, 'Yes, quite' to the notion of a further serving. But 20 per cent, or one in five people, said, 'Not particularly' and another 4 per cent ticked the box marked, 'Over my own grandmother's dead body' (or words to that effect).

Get this, though: 'The standard of the acting was very highly thought of; indeed, in the opinion of some, the acting was considered to have far surpassed the material.' Good to know that we actors had pulled our weight, then, especially given that we were working with material that was evidently beneath us.

Of course, that's unfair on John. You have to bear in mind that the entire first series was written without a single role having been cast or a single scene tried out. It's why comedies so desperately need time – time which today's broadcasters don't have the patience to give them. With the first series recorded, John could now start writing for the characters as they were played. He could have each of us – our faces, voices, bodies – in his head as he wrote. The writing had been unusually strong in the first place. But now it could only get better.

For the second series the title music was changed – from the very typical sitcom theme that had been commissioned from Ronnie Hazlehurst to the now familiar tune and lyric that John wrote (and sang). John had had that music ready for use with the first series but it had been declined. Now, though, people at the BBC saw the value of a tune that in some way helped to explain the series and got people over the hurdle (apparently still a problem) of the obscure title.

Even then, though, the second series performed fairly indifferently. Viewing figures again hovered around the 7 to 8 million mark – and the axe again hovered over the series. John was convinced, from conversations he was having at the BBC, that he was getting gently nudged to ditch *Only Fools*, move on and come up with something new. We'd had two bites at the cherry now. It looked extremely unlikely that anyone was going to offer us a third.

But then came one of those unforeseeable and almost entirely inexplicable developments. The second series was repeated, without fanfare, and its audience began to grow. Shown a second time, it caught on. People began to see what those of us close to the show thought we could see from the beginning: that this was a seriously great set-up. It was the same thing as had happened with *Open All Hours*: the show was saved by repetition.

The lesson being: don't knock repeats on television. They've been very kind to me down the years.

The show raced on from there, and the rest, of course, is history: record-breaking Christmas specials and audiences of 24.3 million that practically stop the national electricity supply in its tracks when everybody heads for the kettle afterwards. Many is the time I have wondered why the programme should have struck so deep and lasting a chord with people. I'm sure someone cleverer than me could write a whole book about that. But I have a small theory about one little thing that might have been a contributing factor.

People often talk about the warmth of *Only Fools* and a lot of that, I'm sure, comes from the fact that there was a small cluster of people at the heart of the show who were sympathetic to the background; who had a relationship with working-class life in London.

John Sullivan had grown up in a small terraced house in post-war Balham, the son of a plumber and a cleaner, and had an upbringing very similar to mine. My background we've already talked about. And Ray Butt, the director, was another London boy who had worked on a stall in the East End with his father. (Ray used to tell a story about how, on his travels as a market trader, he had come across Tommy Cooper, who worked the markets before he found success as a comedian, those two trades having more in common than is generally acknowledged.)

A few of us, then, knew something about what it was like to come from that kind of place, to sense the limited expectations that were laid out for you and to find yourself doing a bit of pushing and shoving to 'get on'. Perhaps that's a small but crucial part of why *Only Fools* rang true and made the connections that it did.

John died after suffering viral pneumonia for six weeks in 2011. I was on holiday in Florida when I heard the news, and being there brought back all the memories of shooting the episode 'Miami Twice' and all that laughter that we had shared. Then I came back to Britain and attended John's funeral and heard and saw all the tributes to him and it was brought home to me again how much he had meant to people and the extent to which this very humble man had made a difference in people's lives.

He was a quiet and unassuming type – never the loudest person in the room, nor necessarily the funniest, but almost certainly the most observant. And I would say he achieved the writer's dream: his work was loved in his own lifetime and he left behind a legacy in the form of a batch of programmes that I feel completely confident will be appreciated for as long as people have devices on which to watch moving images.

Elsewhere, of course, time cannot be made to stand still, no matter how much one would wish it, and the forces of so-called progress are always on the march. You will know, perhaps, that eventually, for reasons we've gone into, the part of Nelson Mandela House in Peckham was played by a tower block called Whitemead House in Duckmoor Road in Bristol. But in the first instance the Trotters' high-rise abode was actually, by the magic of television, a picture of Harlech Tower in Park Road East in Acton.

Imagine my trepidation and despair, then, when I learned that Harlech Tower – the crucible, if you will, of the *Only Fools* story – was slated for demolition, part of a £650 million rejuvenation of the area. Asked to share my opinion of this scheme at the time – the papers coming to me on account, no doubt, of my renowned expertise in matters of urban planning – I said I thought the tower should become a listed building and have a preservation order slapped on it forthwith, effectively saving the building for the nation.

Did they listen? Did they heck.

Since then the gentrification of *Only Fools*-related locations has continued apace. In the summer of 2020, Randalls, the Uxbridge department store, which had been in business 123 years, closed down amid plans to remodel it as fourteen luxury flats. So far as I'm aware, in the discussion of this development, not a moment's thought was given to the fact that, in 1983, during an episode entitled 'Healthy Competition', Derek Trotter had set up shop in the doorway of that very store in order to sell some exclusive, high-quality wind-up dog toys.

Then, with scant respect for entrepreneurial daring, the police turned up, and, to avoid getting nicked, Del had to flee through the store in search of the back exit, where he jumped into the waiting three-wheeler thoughtfully provided by his getaway driver, Rodney – but not before accidentally strewing his suitcase full of hooky dog toys across the pavement.

A legendary site, then. And yet now the place was apparently going to be yuppie apartments with marble bathrooms at £300,000 a pop.

Well, I guess I'm all in favour of people having places to live. But do these planners have no feeling for history?

'Nothing is permanent,' as John Sullivan wrote at the top of that first script. But I suppose I have my memories, at least. And the footage.

CHAPTER EIGHT

On hanging out with the greats, and making the best of the little moments

W as it not the great Greek philosopher Aristotle who said, 'Comedy cannot be taught. It can only be learned'?

No, actually, hang on a moment: now I come to think of it, it was Terry Scott. But no matter. It's all Greek to me. And perhaps to you, too.

Terry Scott's path crossed with mine on three separate and very different occasions along the gently winding and daffodil-lined path of my career, twice quite early on and once much later. Indeed, the first time I ever showed up on the nation's television screens it was alongside Terry. In fact, I wasn't merely alongside him on that formative occasion. I was bashing into him while suspended from a wire.

This was in 1965, in the BBC's annual pantomime, which that year was *Mother Goose*.

This is the moment in the book where you shout, 'Oh no it wasn't.' And I reply, 'Oh yes it was.'

Thank you for your participation.

My part with Terry Scott in that feast of festive televisual fun involved me appearing in an act called 'The Flying Policemen' – a comic interlude, having, I would concede, very little direct relevance to the main thrust of the *Mother Goose* plot, but, by way of compensation, featuring three uniformed constables flying around on wires to music. An airborne ballet, no less, and a reminder, if any were needed, that a vein of daft surrealism ran deep in the light entertainment of the mid-1960s.

Britain remembers Terry Scott most fondly for *Terry and June* and perhaps also for his Dr Prodd in *Carry On Matron*. It remembers him less vividly, quite possibly, for his flying policeman in *Mother Goose*. Yet a surprising number of Terry's earliest roles seem to have been coppers, albeit largely non-flying ones. He was a cop in *Blue Murder at St Trinian's* and again in *The Great St Trinian's Train Robbery* – those wonderful films with the great Alistair Sim.

Terry was also a policeman in *Carry on Sergeant, The Bridal Path, And the Same to You, Double Bunk, What a Whopper* ... in fact, in about half of Britain's comedy film output of the 1960s. Clearly, as far as casting directors were concerned, if you wanted someone to be funny in the vicinity of a truncheon, Terry was your man, and, looked at like this, Sergeant Major MacNutt in *Carry On Up the Khyber* must have felt like a major breakout role.

Terry had also, by the point of our first extraordinary encounter, had an enormous hit single with 'My Brother', a song in which he asked, among many other important questions, 'Who locked Grandad in the loo?' and answered, beyond any question of reasonable doubt, 'My brother.'

Quiz question: what links that legendary Terry Scott recording with my fellow octogenarian, Ringo Starr? Answer: it was produced, like so many comedy records of the sixties, by George Martin, the producer of The Beatles. Musical historians will agree with me, I'm sure, that the flushing loo on 'My Brother' is a direct forerunner of the whooshing noises ('Full speed ahead, Mr Boatswain, full speed ahead') in The Beatles' 'Yellow Submarine'.

But (as Del would say), I digest. My point is merely that Terry was already a big deal by the time I ended up briefly working with him. Indeed, in this 1965 panto he was Mother Goose, the star of the show – and, not to put too fine a point on it, I would argue that none of us was left under any other impression. In fact, I must admit, I was rather struck on that occasion by Terry's somewhat lordly demeanour, which I found quite intimidating. Fair enough: he was the big attraction and the experienced performer, and I was the total new boy, as new to television as I was to police work.

At the same time, slapstick humour is, of course, a great leveller. And slapstick humour when both of you are hanging from the ceiling is even more so. Quite hard to pull rank in those circumstances. Quite hard to pull anything, actually, apart from your own stomach muscles. Yet even in those complicated circumstances for one's individual dignity, Terry somehow managed to make it clear that I was very much the flying beat copper to his flying Chief Constable.

It rather haunted me at the time, that kind of starry haughtiness that makes others in the vicinity feel like lesser mortals, and it certainly made the experience less fun than it probably ought to have been. And correct me if I'm wrong, but being a flying policeman ought to be fun, oughtn't it? Why else would you join the force?

But the sense of awkwardness and mild humiliation that I experienced on that occasion, accompanied by a nagging anxiety about doing something wrong and thereby bringing down on me the scorn of my superior, stayed with me. I was determined that, if I ever reached the giddy standing within the industry of a Terry Scott, I would try to be a bit more friendly and encouraging to people who were just starting out.

The lesson being: be nice to people in the lift on the way up because you might well meet them on the stairs on the way down.

At the time, of course, young, keen and, looking to get on, I bit my lip and quietly put up with the haughtiness. I was just twenty-five. It had been only six months since I had been given my first professional role and less than that since Bromley Rep had taken me on full time at the princely wage of £15 per week. So to be literally hanging out, however awkwardly, with someone of the stature of Terry Scott on nationally broadcast television was ... well, dizzy heights in a very real sense. To be doing so in front of 15 million viewers (for such was the lure of the BBC's panto in those days) was a truly unlikely turn-up.

How did this come about? Those fragile threads again. The panto's producer was David Croft – later the co-writer, with Jimmy Perry, of *Dad's Army*, *It Ain't Half Hot Mum* and *Hi-de-Hi!*, and, along with Jeremy Lloyd, the person behind *Are You Being Served?* and *'Allo 'Allo!* Imagine being the name that links those five smash-hit shows. It's extremely impressive. But at this stage David was a BBC comedy producer and just happened to be one of a relatively small number of people from outside the Bromley area who had seen me perform in Bromley Rep's production of John Chapman's *Diplomatic Baggage*.

Maybe you know the play. It's a challenging but profoundly rewarding piece, set in a vision of a post-apocalyptic future, in which a small cast, dressed in tattered rags, addresses in verse, song and guttural utterance, themes of an existential nature regarding the limits of our shared humanity.

All right, not really. It's a classic British farce in which, owing to the indisposition of the ambassador, a lowly civil servant called Barry has to go to Paris to sign a peace treaty, and ends up in his underwear in his hotel room with a succession of French mistresses and the chambermaid, only to hear from reception that his wife is unexpectedly on the way up in the lift, bringing with her, for some reason, his old and irascible uncle. Which is an existential crisis in its own way, I guess.

In Bromley Rep's production of this classic work, I played the hotel porter – which might sound like a minor role, but actually was a pretty decent one, if I remember rightly, and certainly by my standards at the time. By which I mean I had lines and everything.

Also, I refer you again to the great truth: there is no such thing as a small part, only a small actor. And heed that notion well at this juncture, because in addition to lines in this piece, I also had a bit of business where I was required to enter the hotel room in which our protagonist's farcical philandering was underway, and collect the trolley which I had earlier used to make a delivery of food ordered up from room service.

But now, unbeknown to me, one of the French mistresses is hiding on board the trolley, concealed by a white cloth which extends down to the floor, and is intending to use said trolley as a covert getaway vehicle as the wife's lift draws ever closer. So the trolley now has an extra weight to it that I, the porter, am far from expecting. Which means that when I go to wheel it out of the room ... well, dear

reader, if you're not seeing the potential for comedy may-
hem in this moment then I must accuse you of being a little
behind the pace here, farce-wise.

I certainly saw an exploitable opportunity in that moment
and worked really hard to put together a physical routine
around it – shoving effortfully at this curiously immoveable
object, walking all around it trying to solve the mystery of
its heaviness, eventually pushing at it in such a way that my
legs flew out directly behind me before I crashed to the
floor, and so on.

My spiritual guides as I put this little number together?
Jacques Tati, of course, whose formative impact I have mentioned already. But also Buster Keaton and, perhaps most
strongly of all, Stan Laurel, whom I had adored since the
first time I set eyes on him, which would have been in one
of the Finchley cinemas with my mother. Stan, I eventually
learned, was the brains and the guiding force behind a lot of
the comedy that Laurel and Hardy got up to, and what he
brought to the discussion in that regard was years spent on
stage in British music hall theatres, working live audiences.
His timing, his plotting, his gestures, his feel for what was
funny, his ability to engage with the viewer – all of it came
from putting routines in front of people night after night,
and tweaking them according to how those people reacted.
His were highly theatrical skills in that sense.

Of course, if you wanted to be influenced by Stan Laurel,
you had to join the queue. Dick Van Dyke was one of the

hundreds of others who drew deeply on what Laurel did, and he tells a wonderful story about one day, in the early 1960s, looking through the phone book for somebody's number and, to his surprise, finding Stan Laurel listed there, plain as day, at his home address in Santa Monica. You would have assumed a star as big as Stan Laurel would have been ex-directory by this point in his life, but apparently not.

Van Dyke thought he would at least take the opportunity to ring him and say thank you. He dialled the number and, sure enough, Stan Laurel answered. He knew who Dick Van Dyke was, of course, and Van Dyke was able to tell him how much of a fan he was and also to say that he had taken a lot from him down the years.

'Yes, I know,' said Stan Laurel.

It's interesting to reflect that, despite all those stunts – sitting in cars that fell apart, falling down stairs and chimneys, getting clonked on the head with spoons and worse – the only time Stan Laurel got hurt was in between takes when he unwittingly stepped off a kerb while talking to someone and wrenched his back. As the survivor, entirely intact, of thousands of pratfalls, who is nevertheless a martyr to my own back following a small gardening incident while clearing a pond, I at least have that much in common with Stan Laurel.

Anyway, my carefully planned and entirely unscripted Stan Laurel tribute with the room service trolley seemed to get big laughs, and feeling the warmth of that response coming off the audience when I first tried it out was a proper revelation. It was my first real experience of that level of attention in a proper theatre, and what can I tell you? It was a highly addictive sensation.

What's more, the critics were unanimous. Or at least, the critic in the local paper was unanimous. 'For me, David Jason stole the show,' wrote the man from the *Bromley Times* in one of the earliest reviews in which I had been mentioned by name. (My aunt Ede, whom we met earlier, loyally clipped and kept these early notices in a scrapbook, which is how I still have some of them. I love, by the way, that old-fashioned term 'notices' for what we would now more functionally call 'reviews'. 'Notice' contained so much excitement in it for the budding actor. You were literally getting noticed.)

Get that, though: I stole the show. And our friend in the press seat wasn't wrong to put it that way. It was an act of absolute theft. I can only hold up my hands, guv, and urge you to slap on the bracelets. But why not, if it added something to the show and people enjoyed it? And they can't touch you for it. In fact, it turns out that, if David Croft happens to be in the house to catch you red-handed in this act of theatrical larceny, you get offered work as a flying policeman in the BBC Christmas pantomime of 1965.

Incidentally, there was a third important party in that airborne ballet skit – none other than Jon Pertwee. Again, here was company more distinguished than I had any right to be among at that point. Jon, who was easy-going and funny and to whom I took an instant liking, had already appeared in films, including a couple of the *Carry Ons*, and I had sat with my parents listening to him at home in the radio comedy series *The Navy Lark* (a programme which also featured a certain R. Barker).

In five years' time Jon would know national fame playing Dr Who and if you had put that proposition to him while he was hanging from the roof in a policeman's outfit with me and Terry Scott ... well, he probably would have begged you to summon the Tardis to take him there immediately and get him out of the incredibly painful Kirby harness that all three of us had to wear for this portion of the show in order to be hauled into the skies.

That Kirby harness was pain on a very special level, let me tell you – and, as you know, I speak as someone who (did I mention this already?) once mowed his own toe with a Flymo. The Kirby's twin leather straps, which were passed around the very tops of your thighs, ushered you into a whole new world of agony. After you had been hanging around for a while, those straps began to work upwards in a devious pincer movement, endangering the future of parts of your body that were dear to you and effectively cutting off your blood flow from the waist down. Once you were returned to earth and freed at the end of the routine, it could take your circulation a couple of hours to return to normal and your voice a bit longer than that to drop to its typical frequency.

The lesson being: there is no art without suffering. And certainly no panto without it.

The three of us should have been given danger money – and in a sense, actually, we were. I don't know what Terry Scott and Job Pertwee were on, but the £75 that I earned for three days' labour in the filming of this Christmas entertainment was itself, at that time, the coming of all my Christmases at once. I refer you again to the £15 a week that repertory theatre was paying me in those days. If I didn't know it already, I certainly did after *Mother Goose*: by comparison with repertory theatre, television was the Yukon. There was gold in them thar hills, even when you were working for the BBC.

Anyway, come Christmas that year, the Whites of Lodge Lane gathered in front of their black and white television set to watch, not for the last time, their son appear before the nation at this joyful and important time. I can only imagine how proud it must have made them: there I was – the swinging policeman on the left, dimly visible in a long-shot.

Once the interlude was completed and Terry, Jon and I had finished our dangling, my father turned to me and, fixing me with an admiring look said, 'There's a knighthood in this, son, if you keep going at it.'

OK, he didn't. But there was a tangible sense of wonder in the room – and not just because I had emerged entirely intact from my encounter with a Kirby harness. The fact was, television was another world as far as we were concerned. To my family's way of thinking, the television set was a box in which *people who were not like us* appeared. Yet somehow, as unlikely as it seemed, I had crossed the divide and ended up in there. I think all of us were pretty excited about that, not least me.

My second encounter with Terry Scott was two years after that, in 1967, when I landed a small role, with no wires attached this time, in an episode of *Hugh and I*, the successful sitcom Terry starred in with Hugh Lloyd. That was a show about a bachelor living in Tooting with his mother and a lodger and dreaming up schemes to get rich. Put like that, it sounds a bit like a cross between *Only Fools* and *Sorry!* and I guess that's not far away from what it actually was.

The episode I was in was called 'Chinese Crackers', but beyond that, memory rather fails me, except for my recollection that my part offered me a couple of quite nice lines – ones with the potential for a laugh in them. At least, it offered me a couple of quite nice lines with a potential for a laugh in them until Terry noticed them and their potential for a laugh and had a quiet word with the director. At which point, my quite nice lines with the potential for a laugh in them became Terry's quite nice lines with the potential for a laugh in them.

Reader, be not affronted on my behalf. This is how the business sometimes works, and if I didn't realise it before, I certainly did from that moment on. Still, it was quite an abrupt education at the time for your author in his youthful naivety.

Fate was to bring Terry and I together again a third time a good while later, in 1981. Brian Cosgrove, the presiding genius behind Cosgrove Hall Animations, which was a British studio based near Manchester, asked me to voice the cartoon character Danger Mouse, and they asked Terry to be his hamster side-kick, Penfold.

I must admit, I blanched slightly when I heard it was Terry that they were hoping to pair me up with. Memories returned of the intimidation I had felt in his presence during those previous encounters. But I needn't have worried. If slapstick is a great leveller, then perhaps pretending to be a hamster while someone else pretends to be a mouse is even more so. Or maybe it was just that both of us were in a more comfortable place in our lives. Either way, we now got on like a house on fire. We shared a studio on and off for ten years in the making of that show and it was a very happy project for me.

In fact, looking back now from the rocky outcrop of my enormous maturity, I rate *Danger Mouse* right up there among the programmes I'm most glad that I had the chance to be involved in. Perhaps that might surprise some people. 'What? You rank adding your voice to a children's cartoon among your finest hours?' But I genuinely do.

That's partly because the process of making those shows was so enjoyable. Brian Cosgrove and I were on exactly the same wavelength and it was the start of a close friendship. I had been very lucky in some of the projects I had done in my career up to this point, but I can safely say that I hadn't been involved in anything that felt less like work than those voice-over recording sessions did. It was another of those jobs when you rubbed your head from time to time and thought to yourself, 'I'm getting *paid* to have this much fun?'

Terry and I would do a couple of takes using the script, and then Brian would set us loose to do an improvised version. I have strong memories of Brian at those times, on the other side of the studio glass, collapsing onto the mixing desk with laughter, taking his glasses off and mopping his eyes with a handkerchief. Very often it would be the improvised version that the animators ended up setting the pictures to.

It worked well. The show went out on ITV and there was a point where its viewing figures rose above the numbers watching *Coronation Street*. It had a following in the US, too – something I only really realised a few years back when I went to the American embassy to get a work visa.

The man at the window looked at my paperwork and then looked at me and said, 'Are you the David Jason who played Danger Mouse?' Apparently he had grown up watching those cartoons and he couldn't believe he was now face to face with the actual mouse himself, or at any rate his

At RAF Coningsby in Lincolnshire, presenting a documentary about the Battle of Britain Memorial Flight. I was naturally keen to help, in any way that I could, to mark the occasion and encourage the remembrance of that pivotal event in our history. *(Tony Ward/ITV)*

It was a great honour to be up in the skies filming alongside the magnificent Spitfires and Hurricanes. *(Tony Ward/ITV)*

As a qualified helicopter pilot, flying is one of my greatest passions, and the best thing outside of acting that I ever learned to do. I wish I could fly one of these! *(UK TV Gold)*

I love machines of all kinds. The picture above is from a television series I presented, *Planes, Trains and Automobiles*. Notice that I borrowed the cap from somebody with a large head. *(UK TV Gold)*

On your bike! I have a mechanical brain and I'm often at my most content tinkering in the garage. This is a BSA Shooting Star which I restored years ago.

Here I am in my favourite jacket, which I used to wear on my many diving trips. Didn't think much of the cloakroom attendant on this occasion. Talk about slow . . .

I've been fortunate in my life to have travelled extensively. For the *Planes, Trains and Automobiles* documentary I travelled across the west coast of the US, from Seattle to Los Angeles, meeting some lovely people, having fun, and learning about the machines that made America and changed the world.

Top right: Houston, we have a problem. Not for me. Visiting the Mission Control room at the Kennedy Space Center, where so many historic NASA spaceflight missions took off from, was a pure thrill.

Top left: One of my biggest heroes, and someone who I really look up to – literally! Good old John Wayne.

One of the most special autographs I've signed. Following tradition, I signed a door at the Kennedy Space Center, just like the astronauts do for good luck before they go up in to space.

Here I am just after executing a perfect handbrake turn. The stunt driver was so surprised, and we both found it hilarious.

Researching material for the documentary *David Jason – My Life*, I met up with Larry, Ronnie Barker's son, to look through the artifacts Ronnie had gifted the British Museum. Larry is holding a special charter which Ronnie gave to me upon his retirement.

Let me say this: when I look back at the journey my life has taken, I'm struck first and foremost by how hard it is to believe it, let alone understand it.

Top left: My first school, Northside, next door to where I lived, was an ordinary little school. It just goes to show, you don't have to be bound by your circumstances. Extraordinary things can happen to ordinary people.

Top right: With my close friend Brian Cosgrove, the genius creator of Cosgrove Hall Films who dreamed up Danger Mouse, a cartoon character I was honoured to voice.

A frosty glass, or three. Sinking a few drinks with Bruce Alexander (left) and John Lyons (middle), my fellow actors and verbal jousting partners from *A Touch of Frost.*

My trusted driver and friend Les. We've had so many laughs over the years. I don't tend to drive a Reliant Regal unless I really have to. I prefer something a little more comfortable for the longer journey, if it's all right with you. I think at my age I'm entitled to that.

I really enjoyed the part of Skullion in *Porterhouse Blue*. It was one of my favourites.

Leaning on the gates of the 'Larkin' farm where we had so much fun, with Philip Franks and Pam Ferris from *The Darling Buds of May*. I've not been in anything that looked so consistently wonderful as *Darling Buds*. There's a lesson in there, somewhere. Surround yourself with great people in great environments – a tonic for life.

embodiment on earth. He practically granted me diplomatic immunity there and then.

I spent a lot of time thinking about the kind of voice Danger Mouse should have. Brian had conceived of the show as a kind of cartoon response to the 1960s TV show *Danger Man*, which had starred Patrick McGoohan as a super-smooth British spy called John Drake. I'm not saying there were Bond parallels in *Danger Man*, but Ian Fleming was briefly involved in the show and McGoohan used to introduce himself at the beginning by saying, 'My name is Drake – John Drake.'

Clearly *Danger Mouse* needed to have the voice of a British action hero, in the manner of a quietly spoken and eternally calm Drake or Bond. But there needed to be something softer and more vulnerable about him, too. I wanted to lace a bit of natural human cowardice through the macho, save-the-world heroism because that's what I saw in the drawings and because I thought that was what would make him really appealing to people.

And also because ... well, he was a mouse, and mice are timid creatures, aren't they? Even the ones who get jobs with MI6.

But the thing I most wanted to do was to create a voice that would leave you in no doubt that it was Danger Mouse that you were hearing, and not an actor in a studio (me or anybody else) voicing Danger Mouse. I wanted to eliminate the distinction altogether. You needed to believe absolutely that this particular voice was emanating from that particular body.

My hero and inspiration in this area was Mel Blanc, the great legend of American cartoon voice-overs. From Bugs Bunny to Barney Rubble from *The Flintstones* – now, that's the definition of range, in my book. And in every case, Blanc himself was entirely subsumed in the character. Somehow you never suspected a human of being involved in the creation of Daffy Duck, just as you never thought about Clarence Nash when you listened to Donald Duck. Donald Duck simply spoke like that, no further questions necessary.

What happened to that way of thinking? In some respects we've been living through a golden age of animation – all those fantastic films from Pixar and DreamWorks using sophisticated technologies that we wouldn't even have dreamed of while making those films for Cosgrove Hall. At the same time, I lament what's become of the voices. I remember sensing that the weather was changing some while ago, while watching the part-animated fantasy movie *Dragonheart*, in which no less an actor than Sean Connery had the job of voicing the animated dragon. And every time the dragon opened his mouth, Sean Connery came out. It was as though Sean Connery wasn't acting at all – he was just being Sean Connery. I felt a bit short-changed by that.

It was the same thing, years later, with James Corden playing Peter Rabbit. All I could hear was James Corden's voice coming from the body of a rabbit – a slightly alarming experience rather than a fully involving one. I'm not knocking James Corden. You can be almost certain the producers said to him, 'We want you to be James Corden,' just as I'm sure the producers said to Sean Connery, 'We want you to be Sean Connery.' And, with perfect professionalism, the two of them had gone ahead and delivered, exactly in accordance with the brief. But the main motive here seems to be, not characterisation, but the use of familiar, viewer-friendly voices, and that's not really animation for me. That's another version of 'making an appearance'.

Let me divulge something here, in the hope that it stays between us and you won't pass it on to anyone: but I've often wondered whether, temperamentally, I wasn't more suited to being a voice-over artist than an actor. If your heart's desire is to disappear as entirely as possible inside another character for a while, it doesn't get much better than becoming a cartoon secret service mouse – or Toad in *The Wind in the Willows*, or the BFG in the Roald Dahl tale, which were two other Cosgrove Hall projects that I went on to be involved in, and which are two further pieces of work of which I'm especially proud. Animation is the best way to vanish while still working as an actor – and let's face it, the variety of the roles is potentially unending. Don't let me forget, in that regard, the *Danger Mouse* spin-off cartoon, *Count Duckula*, in which I played the world's first vegetarian vampire duck. You simply don't get those kinds of opportunities to stretch yourself in any other area of showbusiness.

Anyway, it was during that *Danger Mouse* period, when we were in and out of the studio together and occasionally pausing for conversations about the meaning of everything, that Terry Scott bestowed upon me his useful piece of wisdom about comedy, and how it can't really be taught, only learned. The notion confused me for a while, to be perfectly honest, because I sort of thought of teaching and learning as two ends of the same stick. Surely if you could learn it, then you could teach it.

But I eventually worked out what I think Terry meant, which is that you can only really find out what's funny in practice. There are no guaranteed formulas and no theories that you can toss around in classrooms. Up to a point there are tactics you can adopt and maybe some of those can be explained to you. But ultimately the only way to find out whether things are funny is to put them in front of an audience and see if people laugh. It's a constant learning process.

I did my early learning in the theatre and I think I was very fortunate to have that opportunity. Most of the skills I brought to comedy on television were skills I had had the chance to hone for a number of years in front of people in theatres. The stage was where I learned to read an audience and, by extension, it was where I learned everything I know about comic timing. One of the things that most surprised me when I began working every night in repertory theatre was how different each audience could be. It was the same play, in the same theatre, but the difference in the atmosphere from night to night could be enormous. They would bring their mood to the performance just as you brought yours. Each time the curtain went up, the room would feel different, in ways that you wouldn't really know about until that moment. And the skill, I realised, lay in reading that difference and working with it.

You tried to be as aware as you could be of what was going on in those seats in front of you. For example, if it was raining outside, your audience would quite possibly be wet and a bit uncomfortable to start with, so you might want to slow things down a bit and give them a chance to get comfortable – get them warmed up, essentially. You wanted, in as much as possible, to bring everyone along, so if you noticed that there were latecomers you slowed it down a bit, too, to allow them to settle. On Friday and Saturday nights you learned that you had to be firm, not only with your audience but with yourself. Friday and Saturday night audiences would be more relaxed – quite likely more 'refreshed', shall we say, even before the interval, and certainly afterwards. It was the weekend and they would be ready to laugh at anything. But you didn't necessarily want them laughing at just anything; you wanted them to be laughing in the right places. You didn't want to allow them to laugh too long at stuff early on in the play because there was a long way to go at that point, and you didn't want them running out of energy. If they exhausted themselves too early, the back-end of the play was going to fall flat. Ideally, you wanted to be gradually building, shaping the response towards a big pay-off at the end. Big finish, curtain, applause, everybody going home happy – that was the plan.

Of course, what you could never entirely eliminate was the possibility of things going wrong. That was another thing which theatre taught you – a certain amount of nimbleness in the face of the entirely unexpected. I remember when I was at the Strand Theatre in London in a farce called *Look No Hans*, which was written, again, by John Chapman but this time in collaboration with Michael Pertwee, with whose brother, Jon, this chapter found me hanging out earlier.

This was in 1985, when *Only Fools* was gathering pace, and this time I had the lead role as Peter Fisher, a British car salesman working in Berlin and doubling as a fumbling undercover agent. Needless to say, Peter's personal life is complicated by various mistresses, including Mitzi, the voluptuous singing telegram girl, who was played by Anita Graham.

Look, I didn't say it was Shakespeare, did I? And Anita Graham would have known: she was a former RSC actor.

The point is, at one key moment, I was required to make an urgent exit at the climax of a scene where I had been taken hostage at gunpoint, possibly by Mitzi the voluptuous singing telegram girl, although my memory is not entirely reliable here. But what had definitely happened was that at some point in the evening the set on the stage of the Strand Theatre, which would not have been cheap, had nevertheless become slightly warped in the heat from the lights and the door through which we were trying to make our urgent exit was now refusing to open.

There followed a passage of increasingly desperate improvised fumbling. Mitzi couldn't open the door. I couldn't open it for her. It was thoroughly jammed – and so, accordingly, were Mitzi and I.

For a while there it looked as though this scene wouldn't be ending until the carpenter arrived. I could sense the audience growing slightly restless. I racked my brain. Desperate times call for desperate measures.

'Well,' I eventually said, 'there's only one way to get out of here, and that's through the chimney.'

The fireplace had a backcloth on it. I helped my captor into the grate, through the cloth and out the other side. The audience erupted.

The lesson being: sometimes a nimbly corrected cock-up will do more to get a crowd onside than anything in the actual play.

If only that piece of well-received improvisation had happened on the press night. I got a review in *Look No Hans* that stays with me all these years later – a notice, if you like, that I continue to notice. The critic's line was: 'At times David Jason tended to work too hard.'

Hang on, I thought to myself when I first read that: working hard? That's a good thing, isn't it? Why am I getting faulted for working hard? But then I realised what he meant. I was driving the play hard, probably because it was press night, and instead of making it look easy, I had obviously made it look difficult. Point taken, and lesson absorbed.

On other occasions, though, the hard work and the effort to go the extra mile and squeeze the most out of the material didn't look effortful and ended up paying dividends. And perhaps never more so than when Humphrey Barclay of Thames Television came to see me ring a bell in Bournemouth.

On reflection, it was a very similar situation to the one at Bromley Rep with the trolley, actually. But this time the venue for the magic was Bournemouth's Pier Theatre, in the late 1960s, where I was engaged to do a summer season. Again, my role was a relatively small one: I was playing a character called Bobby Hargreaves, who didn't even get onto the stage until after the interval, at the beginning of the second half. The play? *Chase Me, Comrade* by Ray Cooney. Maybe you know it . . . It's a challenging but profoundly rewarding piece, set in a vision of a post-apocalyptic future, in which a small cast, dressed in tattered rags . . .

OK, it's another farce – this time telling the story of a defecting Russian ballet dancer who needs to be smuggled into the house of a British navy commander by the commander's daughter. In the role of the Russian ballet dancer? Dick Emery, whose place in the pantheon of British televised light entertainment was soon to be assured.

Spoiler alert: things become so farcical over the course of the play's next couple of hours that Dick's ballet dancer eventually decides not to defect after all, but to head back to communist Moscow, which had its faults, clearly, but where nobody was trying to stuff him up a chimney, hide him under a sofa, remove his trousers etc. You could sympathise with Dick's character on this score, maybe.

Anyway, once I eventually got on, the set-up was that I was the new person next door, popping in to say hello to his new neighbours but finding himself in a seemingly empty house and wondering how best to announce his presence, and therefore not be mistaken for an intruder. In the middle of the stage, as part of the navy commander's furniture, was a large ship's bell, used a couple of times in the first half to summon houseguests for dinner. All the script really required me to do was to ring that bell, bring the rest of the cast back to the stage and then go on from there.

However, I saw the opportunity for my character to suffer a protracted bout of social anxiety and a wrestling match with his conscience about whether or not he should ring that bell. This crisis of indecision would see me sizing up the bell from afar, nervously approaching it, reaching for it … and then thinking better of it and pulling my hand away, withdrawing to the other side of the room, re-approaching the bell, and so on. If I played this right, and drew it out for long enough and took the audience along with me, I could get people in the audience so agitated that they would be leaning forwards in their seats and shouting, 'Ring the bell! Go on, ring it!' as though it was a Saturday matinee at the panto and there was a school party in.

Humphrey Barclay, a Thames Television comedy producer, had come all the way from London on a tip-off to see me in a play in which I didn't even feature in the first half, and could very easily have got fed up and decided to cut his losses. Indeed, he confessed to me later that he had come very close to walking out in the interval, getting back in his car and going home, and really only the fact that he had travelled so far kept him from doing that. If this theatre had been more conveniently located for Humphrey, he probably would have been tucked up in bed with his cocoa before I'd even rung the bell.

Fortunately for me, his patience lasted just that little bit longer and he got to see me develop that piece of business – develop it further than I had ever dared to develop it, in fact, because I had been told that Humphrey would be in the audience. And just as David Croft had offered me a television role on the back of some slapstick with a hotel trolley, so Humphrey now offered me the chance to be in the children's show *Do Not Adjust Your Set* and opened up the yellow brick road that would lead to me working with Ronnie Barker and all that lay beyond.

The learning doesn't stop, of course, and that goes for everything, not just comedy. I will always watch the programmes that I'm in, whether they are dramas or comedies or documentaries; I try to do so when they go out on the night of their first broadcast. I don't watch recordings, if I can avoid it. I want to see them in the schedules, at the same time that they're being offered to everyone else which, as I see it, is the way that nature intended. Which makes me a little old-fashioned, I know, in the age of catch-up TV and streaming and consuming entire boxed sets in an evening, but it's a habit of watching television that I find hard to shake.

But it also seems important to me from a practical point of view to watch them that way. I guess I'm still trying to get a sense of the audience, the way that I used to in the theatre. I want to feel I'm sitting down and switching on, like any other viewer, and essentially saying to the television screen: go on, then – entertain me. I want to get a sense of how enjoyable the programme is, and switching on when the *Radio Times* tells me to do so is my way of trying to distance myself from the programme so that I can assess it as dispassionately as possible.

What worked? What fell flat? What could have been altered to make it better? How would you go about it if you had another chance? It's not about wallowing in the wonder of your reflected image, as tempting as that may be. There may be moments that make you proud, but, if you're doing this part of the process properly and watching carefully enough, more often than not, it's not an especially enjoyable experience. You're trying to learn from your mistakes, because they're the things that are truly valuable to you at this point.

The lesson being: the only really bad mistake is a mistake you don't learn from.

And sometimes you'll be left making a note to yourself. In my case, if it's a documentary, 'comb your hair' is a disappointingly frequent one. Because on documentaries, unlike on dramas, the chances are there aren't people around whose job it is to tell you to do that kind of stuff.

I've watched pretty much everything of mine when it's gone out. That Christmas in 1965, when I hung from the ceiling with Terry Scott and Jon Pertwee, I was watching. And that night, thirty-one years later, when over 24 million people tuned in to watch the 'Time on Our Hands' episode of *Only Fools* and then rushed for their kettles afterwards ... well, I was one of those 24 million people and one of those kettles was mine.

It will be the same, I don't doubt, every time I'm on the telly. I'm still learning what can't be taught.

CHAPTER NINE

On setbacks, rejections and coming out the other side

Theatre was where I learned about comedy and audiences and picked up so many of the methods that were useful to me when I began to work in television. It was also where I was taught some important lessons about adversity and resilience and where I developed a readiness to ride the knocks and keep at it. This will happen if you end up in pantomime.

Journey with me, if you will, through time's eerie mists to 1979 and the city of Newcastle – specifically to that great city's Theatre Royal where, for the duration of this particular festive season, I am giving my Buttons in an eagerly sought-after production of *Cinderella*.

Bear in mind that at this point, 1979, I am 'TV's David Jason' as far as the publicity material is concerned, but not quite to the extent that I would eventually become 'TV's David Jason'. It is three years since *Open All Hours* went out and semi-sank – and it will be two more years before that first series gets repeated, with more joy, and is recommissioned to greater acclaim. It will be the best part of two years, too, until anybody hears of a programme called *Only Fools and Horses*. I am mostly, as I approach my fortieth birthday, the veteran of a handful of comedy shows that haven't quite flown – shows that I will be discussing, with as strong a stomach as I can muster, later in this chapter.

However, for these glad and tinsel-bedecked weeks I am Buttons. And Buttons – correct me if I'm wrong here – is one of those roles (Lear and Hamlet are others) by which an actor comes to judge himself. Arthur Askey, Tommy Trinder, Tom O'Connor ... so many of the great theatrical explorers have climbed this, we might say, theatrical Everest and have proudly planted their thespian flags at its summit. Setting all modesty aside, I like to think I did the same that year in Newcastle.

Certainly the people of Newcastle were kind enough not to disrupt the performance from outside in the streets, which is more than can be said about the time when Orson Welles was in town. Seriously. In 1951, the mighty American spent a whole week putting his feet to the Theatre Royal's distinguished boards, playing, not Buttons as it happens, but Othello, which, if your agent can't get you work in *Cinderella*, is not too shabby a fall-back.

Apparently though, early on in the run, some musicians insisted on playing outside the theatre during the performance, and the strains of their music were irritatingly audible in the auditorium. Eventually Welles felt obliged to break off mid-play and go out there himself to confront them. Whereupon, using all the diplomatic skills available to him, the great man gave the musicians some money to go away. Which they duly and gratefully did.

The next night the musicians came back and started again. People aren't fools.

> The lesson being: he who pays the piper may have to pay
> him again the following night if he's not careful.

Let me tell you proudly that the 1979 production of *Cinderella* in that same venue was entirely uninterrupted by buskers. Let me also tell you, slightly less proudly, that it obliged me to don a lavishly embroidered, pastel-coloured, twin-piece velveteen outfit, hung with beads, which put me somewhere between a New York hotel bell-hop, circa 1930, and my old mate Ringo on the cover of *Sgt. Pepper's Lonely Hearts Club Band*.

It also allowed me at certain points to cycle around the stage on a bike with a basket and L-plates, again under-scoring the distinction between this special piece of theatre and, say, an RSC production of Chekhov's *Three Sisters*. Or, for that matter, Orson Welles' version of *Othello*, which I believe was entirely bicycle-free.

Opportunity missed there, Orson, my son.

In addition to the bike, a further lavish spectacle had been planned. Sparing no cost, the production had intended to re-unite me on a nightly basis with the undignified agonies of the Kirby harness, for the first time since that night in 1965 when I put on a police uniform and strapped myself in for an evening of light flying next to Terry Scott and Jon Pertwee. The plan had been for me to swoop across the stage in a home-made flying contraption in an attempt to impress Cinders, who was being played by Leah Bell. Cinders, I think, would have been more impressed if, in the technical rehearsal, the harness hadn't sent me zipping across the stage so fast and uncontrollably that I crashed into the set, parts of which would have toppled directly onto the aforementioned Cinders had not some quick-thinking stage hands intervened to hold it all up. The idea was quietly dropped. Thank the Lord. I hated that harness.

Leah Bell, incidentally, was, in addition to being a fine panto actor, a singer on the north-east circuit who ran a Newcastle club where, I was intrigued to discover, for the price of your ticket you would be given, on entry, a stottie, a Northumbrian bread-based snack. Terrific value, surely, and a very popular offer, it seemed. Apparently, people would ring up to ask not who was on the bill that week but what the filling in the stottie was going to be. The stotties always went down well, even if the singer on the stage didn't. There's a decent business model there, I would suggest, for anyone who wants to follow it, as the entertainment industry does its best to emerge gingerly from the Covid-19 crisis.

Anyway, in the absence of that flying sequence, all was going pretty well for me and my bike as Buttons. Indeed, I was cycling to sell-out audiences every night. The show was going over well, and Cinders was getting to the ball without fail, as planned. I was even beginning to understand some of Bobby Thompson's act.

Bobby was a north-east-based stand-up comedian who did a character called The Little Waster. He would come on in an outsized red jumper and a flat cap with a lit fag between his thumb and forefinger, and crack lines like, 'The dole is my shepherd, I shall not work.'

Perhaps you're struggling to remember such a character in the pages of the traditional Cinderella story that you turned as a child, and possibly you're failing to recall anyone smoking a Woodbine in the Disney version, either. And no surprises, if so. Basically, Bobby was coming on and doing his nightclub act at the beginning of the second half, loosely under the guise of being the entertainment at the Prince's ball.

Bashed into the show with a hammer? Maybe, but such, we can surely agree, is the cosmopolitan glory of pantomime when it's done properly.

217

Bobby would walk out with his cigarette, pretending to be the worse for wear, and say, with a leery smile, 'There's a lot of people in tonight. Think of aaal the debt. Ye kna, if it wasn't for catalogues, this place'd be a nudist colony.'

The adults loved it, but I'm not sure what the kids in the audience made of him. Most of it went right over their heads. And a lot of it went right over mine, too, if I'm being honest, on account of the strength of Bobby's Geordie brogue.

'There's a knock at the door. The wife gans t'answer it. "Is Mr Thompson in?" The wife says, "No, but come in. He'll be back soon. Take a chair." "I've come to take the lot," he says.'

Taken at pace, in Bobby's broad accent, this stuff shot past me in a blur of vowels at first. But after a while, my ear got attuned and I began to pick it up better.

So the show was flying, I *wasn't* flying, the audiences were happy and everything was set fair.

But then I had to go and catch a stinking cold. And not just a sniffle – a real humdinger. I'm not sure whence it came. Perhaps time's aforementioned eerie mists were to blame. Or maybe it was the fog on the Tyne. It was certainly the frog in the throat.

I have to insist, though, that doing pantomime with a stinking cold is a unique kind of misery. Maintaining the required levels of theatre-filling cheerfulness while your voice sounds like a station announcer's and your nose is running like an overflowing sewage pipe is, as I'm sure any of the legends of the boards will tell you – Gielgud, Olivier, Branagh – quite a workout for the body, and also for the soul. Doing it while riding a bike only adds another layer of complexity. Again, ask Gielgud.

Anyway, like the pro that I was, I cycled on regardless, right through to the very brief Christmas break. The only day on which the theatre was scheduled to be dark that season was Christmas Day itself. Praise be, as ever, to the essential workers at that time of the year for their sacrifice: nurses, doctors, firemen, people playing Buttons. On Boxing Day I would be required to rise, shine and deliver two portions of my very best panto-performing – a matinee and an evening show – with another six weeks of Buttons to follow that.

There wasn't enough time to return home to London, so I stayed on in Newcastle. I was the only person from the production who did so. Most of the rest of the cast seemed to be local people. Leah and Bobby headed off to the bosoms of their families for the holiday while I headed back to the bosom of my hotel room.

Correct me if I'm wrong, but there are more festive places to spend the night before Christmas than an impersonal city-centre hotel room. No chimney in there, of course, so nowhere to hang my stocking with care, in hopes that Saint Nicholas soon would be there. The best I could probably have done was sit up and wait for Santa to come down the Corby trouser press.

But of course I was feeling really ropey anyway. My plan was to get tucked up and then stay in bed as long as possible on Christmas Day in order, with any luck, to shed some of the effects of this award-winning cold and be ready to leap back into the saddle on Boxing Day. True, spending the day ill in bed would be a miserable way to pass Christmas. But needs must. And maybe in the evening, on Christmas night, I would at the very least mark the season with a dinner of some description in the hotel dining room with a few of the other hotel guests, amid at least some semblance, I hoped, of festive cheer.

So it was that, having risen at about four in the afternoon and dragged myself out for a restorative walk around the city centre's deserted streets (a restorative walk that, as it turned out, didn't restore much), I made my way blearily to the hotel dining room to ask what time dinner was. I was informed by the very nice head waiter that Christmas dinner was between 12 and 2 p.m.

'Surely that's lunch?' I said.

'No, lad, that's dinner,' the waiter replied. It was then I discovered that the catering staff had gone home after 'dinner' and the kitchen was closed.

The duty manager was very kind in the circumstances. She found some cold turkey and some leftovers from the lunchtime sitting, and set me up with a table. And there I sat, on Christmas night, in a deserted hotel dining room, with the persistent remains of a cold, quietly chewing my way through a cold supper and staring out of the window at a dark, wet Newcastle.

What is it that Andy Williams is always saying about 'the most wonderful time of the year'? Not for me in Newcastle in 1979, Andy. I was literally going cold turkey and there was nothing wonderful about it at all.

I regard that Christmas night in the vacant dining room, alone with a stuffed-up head and some cold meat, as probably my personal low point – a moment where searching questions such as, 'What are you doing this for?', 'Is this any way to make a living?' and 'Was it ever like this for Kirk Douglas?' were very prominent in my mind.

In that respect, it nudges narrowly ahead of a number of other low points during my phase as a touring repertory actor, where, in a state of deep despondency, I found myself asking where this was all headed – most memorably while staying in a student tower block down-wind of a chemical factory in Billingham, and on a bench in the middle of a wet afternoon outside Lincoln Cathedral. Those were the times when, at a very low ebb, I was tempted to ponder the meaning of it all and wonder whether, actually, a steady job in electrical fitting would have been the more rewarding option for me.

It wasn't all jollity and frolics out there on the road, is my point. Indeed, even now I partly shudder to recall those English B&Bs of the sixties and seventies – oddly draconian and intimidating places, where additional overnight guests were strictly forbidden on pain of eviction, and where breakfast was served until 9.30 and was certainly not available if you accidentally overslept and got there at 9.31, which happened to me more than once.

Word got around between us travelling actors about the best places to stay – the cheapest, the most liberal, the ones with the nicest and most tolerant landladies, the ones with the best breakfasts. That was handy. You would get off a train at your appointed destination and start ringing around, pushing coins into a phone-box (a practice now largely lost to the world, of course, though it absorbed a good deal of my energy in those days). But when you couldn't get yourself into one of the commended establishments, you simply had to take your chances.

For example, there was one landlady who was famous for extending her hospitality, not just to travelling actors, but also to four cats. I'm not sure whether that technically qualifies as a herd of cats, but it was a very small house so it could seem that way to the visitor. Indeed the whole place would sometimes seem to be a-quiver with fur.

Now, when push comes to shove, I'm probably a bigger fan of dogs than I am of cats, though I can see that a houseful of dogs would present its own problems, too. Nevertheless, cats are fine, as far as I'm concerned. Just as long as they're not in my food.

One morning at breakfast, the landlady put a plate in front of me and, as I eagerly readied my knife and fork, I noticed a thin layer of cat hair across the fried egg. And again that question posed itself: has it really come to this?

Still, 'waste not, want not', as my war-inured parents taught me. I tweezered the hair aside between my thumb and forefinger, discreetly dropped it to join the others on the carpet, and got stuck in.

(That parental lesson on wastage went in so deep that I still repeat the mantra constantly today. Indeed, while reaching into the fridge to retrieve some shrivelled or over-ripe delicacy deemed inedible by everyone else, I only have to begin the phrase – 'waste not ... ' – for one of the other members of my family to sigh and complete it on my behalf.)

I think of that period of my life as the Nylon Sheet Years. The build-up of electrostatic forces in your shiny bed linen would frequently be so great that just to turn over in bed at night was to risk setting fire to the hair on your legs. One had heard, with a shiver, of the electric chair, but this was like being condemned every night to the electric bed, and the chances of waking up fried to a crisp seemed appallingly real.

Those were dark nights of the soul, then – or at any rate, dark apart from the sparks coming off the bed sheets. But I'm sure it's the same for anyone on any career path. There will be these moments when the road ahead looks long and uncertain and is possibly leading to the door of a landlady with too many cats. But at such times you just have to grit your teeth, get back on Buttons' bike and cycle on.

Incidentally, while we're on the subject, it strikes me that, even more than the Reliant Regal, the bicycle has been a crucial mode of transport throughout my professional life – perhaps even its signature mode.

I don't just mean the drop-handle number that I bought for a song off my next-door neighbour, Ernie Pressland, and which I would push down the side passage at Lodge Lane early on dark winter mornings, as an eighteen-year-old apprentice electrician, bound for Fortis Green – six rolls of cable threaded through the handlebars, bag of tools flung over my back, imperfectly protected from the biting cold wind by a donkey jacket and overalls, taking my chances on ice-rutted roads with the trolley buses.

Believe me, those electrical public transport monsters of yesteryear, hooked by roof-poles to their overhead lines, could be a real menace to the innocently bicycling electrician on his way to work. They would creep up in near silence to ambush you, passing you within a hair's breadth. And just occasionally the poles would jump track and spark and flail around like whirling dervishes, at which point you would find yourself cycling into a scene from some kind of movie in which the machines rise up and take over.

If the gritting lorries had been out, you would navigate your way back in the evening through seas of slush, merrily pebble-dashing the lower half of your legs as you went. And please solve this eternal conundrum of the cycling life for me: why are there always more upwards hills on the journey home than there seemed to be downwards hills on the journey out?

Never mind. The point is, I would later find myself on *Open All Hours*, riding Granville's delivery bike – in which I was able to draw on my personal experience of operating a very similar, front-loaded machine for the Victor Value supermarket at the age of fourteen. Ronnie Barker gave me a lovely model of that bike for my birthday one year. Just over thirty years later, I would remount that noble vehicle for *Still Open All Hours* – falling off it in the first episode, in fact, although only in a very controlled way and because the script told me to. Because it turns out that you never forget how to ride a delivery bike.

The lesson being: riding a bike is like ... riding a bike.

In the meantime there had been the unfussy, bone-rattling push-bike on which Skullion, with his pipe clamped in his teeth, rode magisterially through Cambridge at the start of *Porterhouse Blue* and on which he later, in one of my favourite shots from that series, pedalled conspiratorially through the mist and out of town to see Sir Cathcart De'Eath at his racing stables at Coft Castle. Can you pedal conspiratorially? I believe you can. Sometimes a person's whole character can be expressed in the way they ride a bike.

And not that long ago, an edition of the documentary series *David Jason's Great British Inventions* found me trying to mount a Victorian penny farthing. It's a wonder, all things considered, that I've never been sponsored by Halford's.

However, I should meekly confess that my attempt to get on board that penny farthing ended in ignominious failure. Even more than playing Buttons, your penny farthing bicycle really is an Everest to climb. Especially if you're five foot six. I was filming in the company of Tony and Elsie Huntington, a couple of vintage bike enthusiasts, but even with their expert tutelage, I couldn't get into the saddle.

You approach directly from the rear, exactly as you wouldn't approach a horse. You then place one foot on the mounting peg near the back wheel and stretch yourself forward to grab hold of the handlebars, which at this point seem to be about ten feet away – something of a problem for a person of my compact and space-efficient form.

During that giant reach, your nose is basically on the saddle. Or mine was, anyway. Meanwhile you must put all your weight on your left knee, which is roughly parallel with your ear, and in one flowing movement you must project yourself forwards, bringing your groin up and into the seat, preferably without doing yourself an appalling mischief on the way through, and simultaneously engaging your feet with the pedals. Bear in mind that, responding to your efforts behind it, the bike has already started rolling forwards during all this, thus becoming a moving target, which is less than helpful of it in the circumstances.

Honestly, what a palaver. No wonder someone invented the car. My failure to complete this task was nothing to do with age, either. Not even my youthfully elastic, farce-performing, furniture-climbing self would have managed this particular stunt with ease. I took a few stabs at it and then decided to walk away while some semblance of my dignity was still intact. 'Only Fools Star Maimed in Fall from Penny Farthing' wasn't a headline that people close to me were likely to want to read.

> The lesson being: if at first you don't succeed, try, try again – unless it's getting on a penny farthing, in which case feel free to give up.

It's no bad thing to get knocked back, though. It's how you find out how badly you want something and how much you would be prepared to put up with to get to it. I think I can say I know of what I speak in this area – for I speak as someone who was a member of the cast of the massively successful sitcom Dad's Army for ... ooh, at least two hours before he suddenly wasn't.

It happened one day in 1968. In the morning I went to the BBC to read in front of Michael Mills, the head of comedy, and David Croft and Jimmy Perry, the writers, for a role in a new sitcom about the Home Guard in Warminster during the Second World War. At the end of the audition, which went pretty well, I went home and made a sandwich for lunch, whereupon my agent rang to congratulate me because the BBC wanted me to play Corporal Jones, *Dad's Army's* frequently agitated butcher.

Happy days! I permitted myself a little tap dance, figuratively speaking, because this was clearly a massive break for me.

However, barely was the sandwich digested before the phone rang again and my agent informed me that, actually, correction, they didn't want me after all. Sorry, and all that.

Clive Dunn, of course, got that role – and what a job he did with it. But they thought he wasn't available, so they offered it to me. Then it turned out that he was available after all, so I got the chop. And all without even once having had the opportunity to shout, 'Don't panic!'

So that was quite the setback and something of a trial for my resilience. But there were others. After Humphrey Barclay came to Bournemouth Pier and stayed long enough to see me do my big bell-ringing number in *Chase Me, Comrade*, he offered me a place in the cast for a new children's comedy show he was helping develop – *Do Not Adjust Your Set*. This was in 1967. At that point, Rediffusion, who made programmes for ITV, had the title, but they didn't really have the show. That's not always the ideal way to go about doing things, but in this case it seemed to pan out rather well.

Ushered through the door by Humph, I joined a team made up of a young actor called Denise Coffey and some university pals of Humph's – Eric Idle and Michael Palin, who brought along his friend Terry Jones. Sometimes their American mate Terry Gilliam, a hippie in an Afghan coat, would contribute an item or two. From these impromptu and not especially disciplined collaborations a children's show evolved. Each episode was a burst of pure idiocy. Much of it was, on reflection, painfully thin. And yet so are many of the things that kids find irresistibly funny, so it was perfectly targeted in relation to its catchment area.

There was, for example, a skit in which I bopped up and down in the background, looking enthusiastic, while Mike Palin solemnly intoned to the camera: 'This week's guest is David Jason. Next week's guest is ... David Jason. The week after that, we've been lucky enough to get ... David Jason.'

That was it. That was the sketch.

Or there was the moment when Mike said, 'Now David Jason is going to demonstrate how to fall over.' And I duly fell over. And then I got up and fell over again. And again after that. 'Did you enjoy that?' Mike asked the audience. 'I did.'

The thing was, as basic it may seem, this was pretty innovative stuff at the time. Television hadn't yet got round to sending up television, a subject as ripe for satire as any other. And children's television in particular hadn't really let the brakes off before this. It had all been a bit starchy – teacherly, if you like. The anarchy that reliably tickles children hadn't been given free rein in quite this way before. And the show got lapped up. Rediffusion and ITV couldn't have been more delighted. The viewing figures were strong, and the viewers brought in the advertisers. *Do Not Adjust* even won an international award – the Prix de Jeunesse, the first time a show I was involved with had received a decoration. (As my mantelpiece will modestly attest, it would not be the last time.)

The Prix de Jeunesse, though. Bonnet de douche, my friend, bonnet de douche.

Hence the corporate dismay when, after two series, Mike, Terry and Eric decided they wanted to make an adult version of the show. Rediffusion's response was, basically: 'Well, why would we do that? We're on to a winning formula here.' So Mike, Terry and Eric walked away and the show came to an unceremonious halt.

A year later, the three of them, plus Terry Gilliam, were all back on the BBC, along with John Cleese and Graham Chapman, in a programme which was recognisably an adult version of *Do Not Adjust* and which they were calling *Monty Python's Flying Circus*. Maybe you came across it.

No room for me or Denise in that set-up. Indeed, neither of us had been part of the negotiations with Rediffusion over the possibility of changing the show's format, which rather stung us. Mike, Terry and Eric went their own sweet way on that one. So that was a bit of a thumb in the eye. And then the group got back together without us. That gave me a lot to think about for a while, as rejections often will. Those guys were all Oxbridge-educated, and for a long time I had to wonder whether they thought they were a club that I didn't fit into. And maybe they were right. But it was a very uncomfortable feeling, and one which stung me and made me a bit uncertain about myself for a while.

So, *Dad's Army* first and then *Monty Python's Flying Circus*: those were two pretty big planes to watch taking off while you were stuck in the airport. Two monumental and lastingly important pieces of British television history – and I had flirted with inclusion in both of them and ended up in neither. In some ways, it was as though I had been booted out of The Beatles and then gone round the corner and been booted out of The Rolling Stones. I wouldn't have been human if I hadn't felt a bit sore about it – and also a bit worried about what it portended for the future.

Bear in mind that it was several years before I was in anything that was even comparably successful to those two shows. I had plenty of time in that period to wonder whether it was ever actually going to happen for me, or whether those two hours as Corporal Jones were as good as it was going to get, television-wise.

The false starts kept mounting up. When Mike, Terry and Eric walked away, ITV gave Denise and I another children's show called *Two D's and a Dog*. Which was nice of them, but I think both of us ended up wishing that they hadn't.

I mean, I guess it was a sound idea in principle. Denise and I played a couple of youthful amateur crime-fighters and mystery sleuths. Think *Scooby Doo*, but without the animation. We did, though, have a dog. The dog was a giant Old English Sheepdog, of the kind made extremely popular at the time by adverts for Dulux paint.

Indeed, Sheba, as she was known, may well have seen action in a Dulux commercial. She may well even have been a dab hand with the brush and the roller, for all I know. To be honest with you, she didn't talk about it, nor about very much else. Above all, the show seemed to have been conceived as an attempt to cash in on the fondness for Sheba's breed at that time in history. Spike Milligan would have better luck with this a couple of years later, when he starred alongside Digby in the children's film *Digby, The Biggest Dog in the World*. We, frankly, had no luck with it at all.

I have never felt it is good form to talk about other actors' performances and I firmly believe that what happens off-camera should stay off-camera. That said, though – and on the grounds that this is between the two of us, dear reader, and is not to go any further – Sheba was utterly hopeless. Getting her to do anything at the time when you wanted her to do it was difficult – and given that her role didn't really ask much more of her than that she should sit or stand still in the right place, this was extremely disappointing. The damn dog kept wandering off when we were in the middle of our lines. It was almost as though she had a mind of her own and didn't understand what we were trying to achieve.

Denise's character was called Dotty Charles. My character was called (and I wince to remember this) Dingle Bell. Now I think of it, that wouldn't have been a bad name to give the dog. As it happened, Sheba was playing a dog called (hold on to your hats) Fido. The three of us went about the place on a motorbike and sidecar – or at least we did when we could persuade Sheba/Fido to sit in it. In one episode we were employed as ghost hunters by a mysterious Mr Foggitt, played by Bill Fraser. About sixteen years after this, Bill would win the Laurence Olivier Award for his performance in a production of the J. B. Priestley play *When We Are Married* at the Whitehall Theatre in London. I really don't think those giddy professional heights were especially prefigured here. Foggitt was about right.

In another episode, Denise and I were deckchair attendants, which brought us into contact with a seaside comedian called Davy Chuckles, who was played by Norman Vaughan. Not long after this Norman would take over from Bob Monkhouse as host of the legendary gameshow *The Golden Shot*. People forgave him, clearly.

Denise and I struggled, though. The concept was loose and the writing wasn't strong and it was one of those occasions (thankfully rare in my experience) when you know that the show you're making isn't working even while you're in the middle of making it. Accordingly, the energy flopped right out of the thing even as the cameras were rolling.

A publicity photograph taken at the time shows me, Denise and Sheba on a leather sofa. (Yes, the dog was allowed on the furniture, and you wouldn't have wanted to be the person charged with telling it otherwise.) In that shot, I look strangely uneasy and slightly far away, as though a part of me already wishes this wasn't happening. My appearance at that time is also remarkable for an oddly hacked-off fringe – a real pudding-bowl affair. That fringe wasn't the only thing that was hacked off by the end of the six-programmes-long series.

The show went out on Fridays on ITV at 5.20 p.m. Thankfully the BBC's all-conquering *Crackerjack!* was having some time off at this point and Leslie Crowther was resting his pencils. In the context of children's television in the early 1970s, putting a new comedy series up against *Crackerjack!* in the schedules would have been the equivalent of making a short documentary on the origins of pot-holing and scheduling it to go out at the same time as the World Cup final. Still, even then, shorn of competition, *Two D's and a Dog* faded out. That was probably for the best.

Despite that hiccup, Humphrey Barclay continued to have a lot of faith in me. I'll always be grateful to him for that. He thought the show for me was out there somewhere and we just had to find it. That's how I ended up in a comedy series called *The Top Secret Life of Edgar Briggs* – thirteen episodes with me playing a hapless office lackey who accidentally gets promoted above his ability to cope and ends up as the right-hand-man to the head of the British Secret Intelligence Service.

Laughs galore, I assure you – and also stunts galore, to the point, in fact, where the *Daily Mirror*'s critic felt compelled to comment on my remarkable similarity to Buster Keaton, going so far as to credit me with 'most of that great silent actor's gift of timing, rhythm and skill'. Most of it? That was enough for me in that particular comparison.

The show was a critical success, then, but, alas, not a popular one. In 1974 the great British public seemed to find the sight of me falling out of cars and hanging from windowsills strangely resistible. Ditto the sight of me getting my tie trapped in a large suitcase and then accidentally swinging the case destructively into a dressing table. And ditto again the sight of me landing face-first on a decorator's papering table. They certainly preferred the sight of *The Brothers* on BBC1, the established Sunday night drama series against which *Edgar Briggs* was ambitiously pitched. It would have been safer to go up against *Crackerjack!* There was no contest. Edgar lost.

The failure of that show to spark popular approval was a big come-down for me. I had really been persuaded in the build-up that we were on to something. But it wasn't to be. I felt equally confident about another of Humphrey Barclay's gifts – *Lucky Feller* in 1976. That show was brilliantly written by Terence Frisby, who was responsible for the play

There's a Girl in my Soup, which held the record for a West End comedy run (2,547 performances) until (excuse me while I gently clear my throat here) *No Sex Please, We're British* overtook it (6,761 performances).

In *Lucky Feller*, I was a character called Shorty Mepstead and the set-up was a love triangle between me, my older brother (played by Peter Armitage) and my fiancée (played by Cheryl Hall). I thought it was funny and plausible and tightly constructed. If only a few million more people had agreed. Again, though, viewers were not exactly climbing over each other to get to the television set and the show was put away after one series.

In between those two there was *It's Only Me – Whoever I Am*, the Roy Clarke show which I already talked about and which got no further than the pilot. Three strikes, then. I had to wonder whether I was out.

Meanwhile, just to tip a big old portion of Saxa into the wound, *Dad's Army* and *Monty Python* were going from strength to strength. I could be forgiven for sighing deeply about that in quiet moments alone. Of course, it would come good for me in the end. In the meantime, I left my flat one day, walked round the corner and bumped into a little film shoot going on, right there on the pavement. This must have been around 1972. Some people were making a commercial. A man was standing over a crate of dog food and talking to a camera. It was Mike Palin, extolling the virtues of Hunky Chunks – 'the moist, meaty dog food that contains more concentrated nourishment than canned dog food'.

Far be it from me to sneer. Why, I myself that very morning was probably on my way to a voice-over studio to lend my vocal talents to a throat lozenge or a supermarket chain or whatever other item needed it and was willing to pay. But I must admit, in the circumstances, I got a kick out of ducking into a doorway and then sliding out to catch Mike's embarrassed eye.

I always raise my eyebrows a bit when people look back across their lives and say, 'I wouldn't have changed a thing.' I find myself thinking: really? Not one little thing? Not one little aspect that you wouldn't have minded working out differently? In my case, I wouldn't have minded finding out what would have happened if I had ended up in *Dad's Army*. What would that have felt like? What would I have brought to the role? I'm still curious to know.

True, it's perfectly possible that it wouldn't have been a great thing for my career. I talked before about how a role in a successful sitcom can cement you in place. You could argue that Corporal Jones would have taken up so much of my time, and put such a stamp on me, that I would never have got the chance to play Del, or Pa Larkin or Frost or any of the other deeply satisfying things I ended up doing. It happened to a lot of the cast of *Dad's Army*. Those characters embedded themselves so deeply in the public imagination that people struggled to think of the actors behind them as anyone else. It was a force beyond their power to change.

The crucial thing was realising that those opportunities had gone and that there was no point in dwelling on their loss. Rather than sit around feeling miserable about what might have been, I had to pick myself up, dust myself down and look for other things to do. I had to make sure those missed chances weren't the end of something, but the beginning of something else. I'm not saying that was always easy, but it was the way it had to be done.

But even now, if I had the magical power to do so, would I go back and entirely remove all the bumps along the route so that the path of my career ran entirely smoothly? I'm not sure that would be wise, even if it were possible. Those bumps, you eventually realise, turn out to be the things that make the journey a journey. In many ways, it's not during the big, successful moments that you prove yourself, it's during the knock-backs and the upsets. That's when you find out what you've got. And in due course you work out that the successes, when they came, weren't just better for those knock-backs – they were built on them.

The lesson being: it's not the arrival that matters, it's the journey.

The great comedy duo Morecambe and Wise were famously asked in a television interview, 'If you couldn't have been comedians, what would you have liked to have been?' And without even pausing, Eric Morecambe replied, 'Mike and Bernie Winters.'

I don't have a sharp answer to that question. If I couldn't have been an actor, I know what I would have been, because I already was one: an electrician. But what would I have liked to have been? There's nothing. I became the thing I wanted to be. And I understand now that it was *because* of the times that things didn't work out, and not despite those times.

CHAPTER TEN

*On eating nicely, swallowing your pride,
and the recipe for a perfick life*

M y lockdown pastime? Well, when I wasn't staring out
of the window in the forlorn hope of playing 'count
the passers-by', or cementing my claim to be an online
'influencer' with my home-shot Trigger's broom infotain-
ment clip, I filled a few of those long and vacant hours in
the spring and summer of 2020 watching *Blue Bloods*.

And there was a lot of it to watch, if you chose: ten series
and more than 200 episodes and counting. *Blue Bloods*, in
case your own lockdown didn't cause you to venture that
way, is an American police series, revolving around the fictional Reagan family, who all seem to be involved in law
enforcement in some way or other. Frank Reagan, played by
Tom Selleck, is the head of the family and is the New York
police commissioner. His dad was a policeman before him,
one of his sons is a detective, the other is a cop in uniform,
and his daughter is a district attorney.

And at least once in almost every episode the whole family will get together for dinner around the table, no doubt starving from all that work bringing people to justice in various ways ... and hardly anybody will eat. There will be food on the table, all of it perfectly edible-looking, but you can practically guarantee that everyone sitting down will be being very picky about actually getting any of it inside themselves. It's apparent that this powerful and extremely busy crime-busting family, contrary to every other impression, runs entirely on crumbs and air.

Forgive my eagle eyes, but I'm afraid the upshot of spending as much time as I have on the other side of the camera is that you turn into a bit of a spotter for the way that budgetary and time constraints reveal themselves in the shooting of television programmes.

Another big give-away: the three-way conversation where everybody sits still throughout. There will often be a good reason for that. As soon as someone moves, money will have to be spent because time and labour will be needed to re-light the set. Quicker and cheaper just to plonk everyone down and leave them there. You will see these constraints in operation frequently in fast-turnover series, mentioning no episodes of *Midsomer Murders*.

But mealtimes are their own particular category of problem. When you are cutting from camera to camera around the table in a meal scene, the continuity tends to get horribly complicated. Exactly how much of that plateful had each character demolished before we left off to shoot this same scene from another angle? What level were all the drinks at? Exactly how big was the mouthful our main character was in the middle of chewing through?

The best approach for the actor, continuity-wise, is to get a tiny bit of food on the edge of your fork and gesture with it in the close-up shots, saving any actual eating you're going to do for the wide shot where there is less attention on what you're getting up to. You'll see an awful lot of gestures made with loaded forks in television dramas if you look out for them, as I hope you now will.

Or better still, don't eat at all, which seems to be the favoured solution of Tom Selleck and his crime-cracking family. Fair enough. I understand your pain, Tom. In a televised supper, in the course of eating one sausage, what with the different takes from different angles, you can end up eating four. This is no business for faint hearts, nor faint stomachs.

Now, obviously there are a number of other more fundamental contrasts between *Blue Bloods* and *The Darling Buds of May*, the ITV H. E. Bates adaptation from 1991. But *Darling Buds* was a series in which *everyone* ate, and for real. Continuity problems, be damned.

And especially my character. Pa Larkin had to really enjoy his food. It was the key to his nature. He had to tuck in, get that sausage properly eaten. Or all four of those sausages, as it often turned out, once you had done the various angles. By the end of a day's shooting, I could be groaningly full of sausage. And also of fish, and of chicken, and of potatoes, and of ham sliced thick and slapped between big slices of white bread ...

I put on over a stone filming that series. It made a bigger man of me, in the most literal of senses. But thus do we actors suffer for our art. Didn't Robert de Niro do something very similar in order to play the boxer Jake LaMotta for the post-retirement scenes in *Raging Bull*? It's known as method acting, and I'm a big fan of the approach. Especially if it involves eating ham sandwiches. Although Bob's chosen tactic on that occasion (apparently he took himself off to Italy for a couple of months before filming started and ate a lot of pasta and ice cream) also has a lot to recommend it, if your budget permits.

Not for the Larkins, clearly, that old-fashioned and slightly contradictory English notion of politeness around food – one that I was definitely raised under – which, on the one hand, believed that frugality was a good thing and yet which, on the other, insisted that there was something a bit improper about finishing absolutely everything on your plate. To do so might imply that you hadn't been served enough, which would be deemed rude of you. 'Leaving a bit for Mr Manners', we were taught to call it. It was considered impolite to clean your plate, or certainly when you were in company.

And it was considered particularly impolite to clean your plate by picking it up and licking it, but that's another matter.

And not for the Larkins any lack of generosity about portion size. Which makes me wonder how they would have reacted to a hotel I used to stay in in Weston-super-Mare, back when I was a repertory actor and doing summer seasons. I went to Weston for three successive years in the 1970s, on at least one of those occasions appearing in the Brandon Thomas farce *Charley's Aunt*, and because I stayed in the same hotel each time, I got to know the bloke who ran the place. His name was Bob Cutler and he and I became good friends – so much so that sometimes on a Sunday evening, my only night off, I used to go out in the kitchen and help plate up the evening meals for his customers. I liked being helpful and we both made it entertaining – while keeping it strictly hygienic, of course.

Bob was obviously grateful for the assistance and no doubt recognising me to be a responsible sort of person and clearly capable of rolling up my sleeves and taking on the bigger challenges, he put me in charge of serving the peas.

Simple, I thought, as I spooned them out with generous abandon. But within seconds I was getting reprimanded.

'No, you don't do it like that ... ' said Bob.

'What's wrong?'

'No, no: you need to *lean* them.'

'I need to what?'

245

'You need to *lean* the peas.'

Taking the spoon, Bob took a dip into the saucepan and removed what, to my eyes, looked like a fairly negligible quantity of peas. And then, sure enough, just as he suggested, he set those peas down very carefully on the plate and, using the spoon as a kind of ... well, leaning device is probably the best way I can describe it, he leaned them up against the potatoes.

'Makes the serving look bigger and more appetising than just flat on the plate,' he explained.

At this point, suspecting a wind-up, I was looking round the room for the people from *Candid Camera*. But then I looked down at the peas. And blimey – he was right. Uncanny. It was an optical illusion worthy of David Copperfield. When the peas were leaned against the potatoes, it looked like there were more of them. You seemed to be getting more peas for your pennies than when they were slapped down on their own, unleaned. Boundless savings on peas, I guess, and countless satisfied diners who probably reminisce to this day. 'Do you remember that hotel in Weston-super-Mare? Lovely place. And so generous with the peas.'

Does Gordon Ramsay know about this? Someone should tell him.

Still, pea-leaning? Ma Larkin, passing those heaped platefuls down the table, with whole haddock hanging off them, would not have approved, nor even understood, really.

Looking back across the landscape of my career in all its magnificent immensity, I realise that food has been the gift which kept on giving. It's the comic actor's friend, if you treat it right. Seated at the tea table in the aforementioned Weston-super-Mare production of *Charley's Aunt*, I would stuff whole lettuce leaves into my mouth to exploit the comic possibilities inherent in trying to conduct a conversation with people while trying to ingest large lumps of salad. I would look like a giraffe with half a branch sticking out the sides of my mouth.

That's when I wasn't using a spoon to catapult sugar-lumps off the tablecloth into teacups. (You could get a round of applause if you got that one right. And you got a laugh if you overshot and got it wrong. Win-win. In fact, I transferred that little routine to a relatively recent episode of *Still Open All Hours*. It got a round of applause there, too.)

I was still at it in *Only Fools*: picking up a chicken leg, for instance, in that episode where Del and Rodney end up at a posh shooting party, biting into it with relish, using it to gesture a little too closely to my appalled host's face and then plonking it down in the fruit display.

The lesson being: what's the point of a meal if you don't make a meal of it?

And I was back at it again in *A Touch of Frost*. The first time we see Frost in the police station in episode one, he's got a bacon sandwich held aloft above his head like a trophy as he makes his way against the flow up a crowded staircase. No plate for it, of course, because that would be far too fussy and civilised. And once he's in his office he takes a huge bite out of it and a mighty glug on a mug of tea – a mug of tea with actual tea in it, by the way, because I think you can always tell when actors are pretending to drink from empty cups. The cup has no weight to it and the actor's mouth, as it takes its fake sips, ends up looking all wrong. Fill the cup, I say, and drink deep from it.

And I speak as someone who, if I may be so immodest, has developed his own little area of mastery here, in the business of consumption on camera. At any rate, I once had a letter from an American director who had seen a couple of episodes of *Only Fools* and who wrote to me specifically to commend me on my ability to act and eat at the same time.

I'm not kidding: the way that I could demolish a bacon sandwich while making myself crisply audible and yet without spraying breadcrumbs the length of the room drew awed appreciation from the other side of the pond. Needless to say, that letter was the beginning of an enormously fruitful and mutually satisfying working relationship that saw me appear in a string of Oscar-nominated Hollywood action movies.

Wait: no; I've just checked, and it didn't actually. But apart from the last sentence, the above paragraph is entirely true. What can I say? Working efficiently with foodstuffs is simply a talent that I have cultivated, and one that has served me well down the years, through *Only Fools* to *Darling Buds* to *Frost* and all stations in between. The obituary writers will always have that, I guess: 'He was the leading actor of his generation when it came to falling through a bar-flap. And he knew how to stuff his face on camera.'

At the same time, maybe I shouldn't brag too much. I also once had a letter wondering why I always had to be eating like a pig every time I was on the telly. For this correspondent, at least, the argument about justification on the grounds of realism seemed to be holding no water.

The letter, by the way, was very neatly written. In block capitals. By someone who was apparently pressing the pen down very hard. And with no return address supplied. What did they think I was going to do in response? Go round and eat in front of them?

Anyway, in at least this one sense, maybe I had been preparing all my life to play the part of Pa Larkin. The Larkin family was all about taking pleasure in life, and at the heart of that was taking pleasure in eating. Long before *Darling Buds* was adapted for television, it was a radio show – *Just Perfick*, a 1969 series with Bernard Miles and Betty Marsden. And even in the promotional photograph for that radio version, Betty as Ma is carrying a huge roasting tin with a fat turkey in it, while Bernard, voicing Pa, stands alongside holding a pie the size of a motorbike helmet. Food was just the simplest visual shorthand for what the

Larkins stood for – an ample, generous domestic life, lived to the full.

Still, as much as Pa Larkin and I seemed bound by fate, and much though there is ambition and drive and planning involved, most people's acting careers are at least in part a lucky cascade of the dominos, and mine was no exception. I got to be in *Darling Buds* because I got to be in *A Bit of a Do* in 1989. And I got to be in *A Bit of a Do* because I had been in *Porterhouse Blue* in 1988. This was the portion of my career when *Only Fools* had become ragingly successful and when – despite my delight at that outcome, and for reasons aforementioned – I was working as hard as I could to put some distance between myself and Derek Trotter.

In this line of work, you can carry a reputation around with you that's often based on the most recent or most prominent thing that you have done, rather than on things you did before that most recent thing, or things that you might be capable of if given the opportunity. It's the most difficult thing to manage because it's not entirely in your control. Potential is the hardest thing to quantify, and the riskiest. People inevitably end up casting you based on what they have already seen you do, meaning you get funnelled in certain directions, whether you like it or not.

If your ambition is to show your versatility and play a wide range of parts, you are necessarily going to find yourself pushing back against that tendency, which is not always easy, and not if you want to stay employed. When I was in that position, with the character of Del Boy tending to enter any room along with me, the only thing I could do was to keep fighting it and to make sure that I gritted my teeth and jumped through any extra hoops that people set out for me.

For instance, when I went to audition for the part of Skullion in *Porterhouse Blue* (a four-part adaptation by Malcolm Bradbury of Tom Sharpe's novel, made for Channel Four), I wasn't just made to read for the part. I had to leave the room and get into costume – put on Skullion's waistcoat and bowler hat and his pin-striped trousers. Then I had to go back into the room, dressed for the part and read again. That hadn't happened before. But I think I know what it was about. The producers were having trouble conceiving of me as a character other than Derek Trotter, and they needed the visual proof that I genuinely could turn up and put them in mind of someone else. I possibly had to go the extra mile in order to settle a few nerves about it all.

Perhaps some leading actors would have balked at that extra dressing-up requirement. Frankly, some actors, at a certain level, would have balked at even *reading* for the part. 'You ought to know what I can do by now: either offer me the role or don't,' would be their attitude.

But I didn't see it that way and I wasn't too proud to prove myself if asked to do so. And I'm glad I wasn't, because it worked out OK. I got the job, and playing Skullion opposite Ian Richardson's Sir Godber Evans and with John

Sessions as Zipser was one of the most exciting and rewarding things that I ever got involved in. People still talk about that drama very fondly, all these years later – and I'm one of them. It was a totally different part for me – a straight role in a comedy – at exactly the point in my life when I was most worried about getting penned in or typecast. And (permit me to mention) it won me a BAFTA that year for Best Actor – a huge endorsement which, I must say, went a long way towards banishing some anxieties I had been carrying with me, as an untrained 'self-starter', about whether I was doing this acting thing 'right'.

One thing I had in my favour after this was that I had the belief of David Reynolds at Yorkshire Television. It was David who offered me the chance to be in *A Bit of a Do* – a set of hour-long comic plays written by David Nobbs and shot with no audience or laughter track – which was an opportunity I seized. Even after *Porterhouse Blue*, I remained conscious of the need to keep creating spaces between myself and dear old Del when I could. After all, *Only Fools* was carrying on through all of this, and not seeming to grow any less popular or to exert any less of a fascination for people.

So, in that respect, Ted Simcock in *A Bit of a Do* was just the ticket: a northern man on the rise, a pillar of the community and a leader of industry, as he saw himself, although by that he meant the director of a company that made custom-built door-knockers and fireside 'companion sets'.

Either way, there was nothing very Trotter-y about him. That said, there was a slightly risky moment in episode one where the families were lined up for the traditional group wedding photograph, and Ted, in his self-appointed role as ice-breaker, decided to shout 'fromage' instead of 'cheese', as instructed – a moment which might have risked raising the ghost of Del a little incautiously. But I seemed to get away with it.

Coincidentally, in the very first shot of the series, I'm on the phone with a sandwich in my hand, eating and talking at the same time – those crucial skills again. Yet, in Ted, I was playing a character who gets the woman, which was something of a theatrical first for me. The delicious set-up in the opening tale of the series was that the father of the bride and the mother of the groom end up copping off with each other at the wedding reception. This steamy liaison put me in the unusual position of having Nicola Pagett sidle up to me while I was standing with a plate of sausage rolls (food again) and whisper, 'I ache for your body.'

Which nobody had ever said to my character in a drama before, whether he was holding a plate of sausage rolls or not. Actually, come to think of it, nobody had ever said that to my character in real life, either.

Nicola would further report, *sotto voce* and with smouldering intent, that she was 'aflame with sexual hunger' – a hunger beyond the capacity of sausage rolls alone to assuage,

253

clearly – and soon after that the pair of us were relocating to a conveniently unoccupied hotel room where, in front of possibly the widest eyes I have ever pulled on behalf of a British television audience, the enflamed Mrs Rodenhurst was gently dropping her basque to the carpet.

Think of the Mrs Robinson seduction scene with Anne Bancroft in *The Graduate*, if Dustin Hoffman's Benjamin had been a number of years older, married and a northern ironmonger.

But what a privilege to be a part of this set-up, and shaking up a few preconceptions. And what a privilege, also, to be alongside a very young David Thewlis, playing my slightly useless-seeming son, tie askew, jacket too short for his arms. I was fond of the moment in the church at the beginning of the wedding service where, with the bride having made her entry, I had to nudge him to get up and go to the altar. It was one of those little details that spoke volumes. Soon after this, David would have film offers coming out of his ears, a situation that continues to this day. And the rest of us would still be waiting for the phone to ring. No hard feelings, though.

After *A Bit of a Do*, it was the trusty David Reynolds again who was able to point me in the direction of Pa Larkin. Pa was another 'step change', as we might now say, from Del, although, of course, both of them shared a very similar mindset when it came to matters of taxation. Another Jason stock-in-trade seemed to be emerging: first people who cheerfully stuffed their faces, and now people who didn't mind fiddling the Inland Revenue.

Ironic, really, given the circumstances and my own ingrained attitudes to these things. I still have the little notebooks in which I painstakingly wrote up my earnings as a jobbing actor and still recall the almost neurotic anxiety with which I carefully set aside the correct proportion for Mr Taxman when he should come a-calling.

But then my home background was fundamentally a training in careful economics, I now realise. 'Earn a little, spend a little, save a little,' was the mantra at home, and it was drilled into me, along with all that necessary post-war frugality: switching lights off, shutting doors to stop the draught, eking out the coal on the one and only open fire my parents permitted themselves at any one time. Did I mention that ice used to form on the *inside* of my bedroom window? If it hadn't been for my father's wartime greatcoat, I honestly think I would have frozen to death a long time ago.

When electricity finally arrived at Lodge Lane, replacing the gas light, we had a meter that was fixed high up on the wall in the hall. I can still vividly recall standing on the newel post at the foot of the stairs in order to reach that meter and feed it with shillings. Pumping coins into a box to prevent the lights from going out will tend to cement in your mind the link between electricity and expense, and in my case the link held firm. I still go around turning off lights in empty rooms today – to the bafflement, I might say, of other members of my close family, but what can I do? It's a reflex.

Still, here I was embodying a man who famously declared (and to a tax inspector, too) that he only wished he earned enough to be able to afford a luxury like tax. That's not a line I've ever tried to run past my accountant. Again, though, we return to our theme: the joy of acting is above all the chance it gives you to escape from yourself.

Much like with *Only Fools*, none of us had a real concept of the extent to which *Darling Buds* would catch the national mood and leave a lasting impression on people – a lastingly warm impression. When I read the book and looked at the scripts, I loved them both, and I really relished the prospect of playing Pa – playing a character who wasn't neurotic or anxious, for once, but who simply took the world as he found it. But I had a nagging worry that there wasn't enough action in it for the story to convert happily to television, or certainly in such a way as to pull big audiences. I could imagine it going out quietly in an undistinguished slot, to a small gathering of dedicated fans, and with people using that killer term 'gentle' about it.

Obviously I was wildly wrong about that – as evidenced by the fact that more than 18 million people tuned in every week during that first series, and the seemingly invincible *Coronation Street* was briefly nudged aside as ITV's most-viewed programme. I hadn't anticipated how much the series would create an immersive world – that it would build a place that people wanted to disappear into.

Partly that was about the writing, and partly that was about the look of the show. I've not been in anything that looked so consistently wonderful as *Darling Buds*, which was so carefully lit at every turn, inside and out, and shot on film stock, which ensured that the quality of the light wasn't lost. It was sumptuous to look at. It beckoned you in.

And, of course, it was about the characters. The Larkins were quite poor financially, really, yet bottomlessly wealthy in spirit and in heart. They were unconstrained by convention, unashamed of their appetites – for food, drink, love, sex. Pa Larkin was an epicurean, a sensualist, in love with the Kent countryside all around him, with its bluebells and its strawberries and its nightingales, yet also a mixer of cocktails with knockout potency. He and Ma formed this entirely sympathetic union in which they became the enemies of everything that was pretentious and starchy and cautious, and they seemed to point a way to happiness through pleasure in what you had, and delight in the moment, and just basically relaxing about everything. If only that philosophy was as easy to obtain and live by in the must-have, consumer-driven world we currently inhabit.

It struck a loud chord with people. As H. E. Bates himself once wrote about the Larkins: 'They live as many of us would like to live if only we had the guts and nerve to flout the conventions.' The Larkins think, as Bates also memorably put it, 'through the pores of their skin'. It's not by any means given to all of us to be able to do that, but watching the Larkins, you could feel that you were at least being nudged a little further in that direction.

> The lesson being: ask yourself what Ma and Pa Larkin would do. Unless you're talking to your accountant, obviously.

Could the Larkin family be about to strike that loud chord again? As we tentatively explore this sensitive question, come with me, I bid you, on one of my rare public excursions beyond the walls of Jason Towers and out into fame's glossy limelight. In January 2020, when our part of the world was still free to gather together in blissful pre-Covid ease, I went with Gill and Sophie and one of Sophie's pals to the premiere of the Cirque du Soleil show *Luzia* at the Royal Albert Hall.

Pretty good, thank you for asking. I love a Cirque du Soleil show; so much, in fact, that I'll even run the gamut of the dreaded red carpet, showing my best side to the cameras of the assembled press, if it means I get in to see one for free.

Such surreal occasions, though, those premieres. It's certainly a rare day, in my experience, when Peter Shilton, the former England goalkeeper, comes up to say hello. I also bumped into Hugh Dennis and was able to tell him off for stealing all my voice-over work – for stealing *everybody's* voice-over work, in fact. The next minute I was sitting down next to Myleene Klass. And the minute after that she was taking my daughter and her friend off to meet Gemma Collins from *The Only Way Is Essex*, which they were very excited about. It was just like any other Tuesday night in the pub, really.

And, of course, there were selfies. These days, there must always be selfies. Which is fine, but I must say, I rather miss the old days of the autograph book. Back then you would be signing someone's proffered page (frequently lilac-coloured, for some reason) and you would ask them who else they'd got.

'Sinatra.'

'Really? You've got Sinatra? Show me.'

And they'd peel back through the pages to reveal it. That was fun. And certainly as close as I got to sharing a stage with Frank.

OK, it didn't happen all that often. And, thinking about it, an autograph book dropped onto your dinner plate in a restaurant when you're not looking for it is possibly even more dislocating than a request for a picture. But I preferred to be involved in that kind of exchange, by and large, than to be standing and looking gormless for someone's phone-camera. I may be battling against the current here, though.

And then there was the bloke at the Albert Hall who introduced himself to me as a great fan of my work and had all sorts of questions for me, while I sat there waiting for the lights to go down and the show to begin. Extremely flattering.

Then he further revealed that he was a freelance journalist for one of the tabloids. By which time, of course, I had unguardedly told him five stories about Michael Barrymore.

No, not really. I don't know five stories about Michael Barrymore. Sneaky ploy, though.

Is Del Boy coming back? Is Pa Larkin coming back? These were among the questions, as they always are. I start to feel like I'm in the reincarnation business. This time, though, there did seem to be some substance to at least one of the rumours that was being lobbed at me by my 'fan' for my reaction.

Now, you always have to be careful around those stories about programmes which are 'slated' to be coming to your screen soon, and about the stars who are 'slated' to be appearing in them. I know from experience that those rumours can often be a kind of 'trial balloon' sent up by broadcasters or producers to see what the reaction would be to the idea.

If people jump on the story enthusiastically, then the producers know they're on to a good notion and should probably go full steam ahead. If, on the other hand, people seem to be implying that they would rather perform their own dental extractions than eventually tune in, then the idea can be quietly shelved for another time, or no time at all. It's a very cheap and convenient way to test the water.

However, it did seem to be the case that ITV were indeed, at that point, planning to re-make *The Darling Buds of May*, with Bradley Walsh as Pa Larkin and Joanna Scanlan in Pam Ferris's old role as Ma. And I think the assumption of my interviewer (without wishing to pre-judge anybody) was that I might have a fairly strong reaction to this particular piece of news – a strongly proprietorial one, perhaps.

As, indeed, I did. I told my new friend exactly what I thought about it.

And what I thought about it was this: that it was a fantastic idea – that it might even, if it happened, and if it worked, connect us all back to a kind of television that had fallen out of favour, and rather sadly so, from my point of view.

There. That took the wind out of his story.

Or maybe not, as it happened. Cue a headline in our friend's tabloid: 'Sir David Jason backs the *Darling Buds of May* remake, slams vulgar TV shows'.

And cue a story which began: '*Only Fools and Horses* star David Jason has criticised current TV shows for being too vulgar and is in favour of a comeback for more family-friendly television.'

Well, I wasn't sure that, during that conversation at the Albert Hall, I had 'slammed' anything. Quite apart from anything else, the Albert Hall is rather posh. That's why they call it the *Royal* Albert Hall. They rather frown on 'slamming' there.

However, in good old British tabloidese, of course, to 'slam' something is to raise an eyebrow at it ever so slightly, or register a mild objection towards it. So, in that sense, maybe I was guilty of some slamming in London's most dignified auditorium that night.

But I meant what I said about television. It's just a fact of life that today's programmes favour the hard-hitting, the callow, the angry. There's an increasing harshness to things – not entirely, of course, but broadly speaking. Fashion and commercial pressures alike encourage the extreme. The tone is louder, more shouty. There's less sense of television as an entertainment that we sometimes gather together for as families, and more sense of it as something consumed individually, in our own time and at our own pace. I don't think I'm saying anything controversial here: it's not the great unifier that it once was.

And in that, of course, television only reflects life more generally. There's a tendency towards harshness and division that you can notice almost everywhere. You have to be careful how much you bash on about this because you end up sounding crustier than last week's French bread, but social media has an awful lot to answer for in this area. It fuels a certain kind of debate with a certain kind of tone, and all with such ease.

Back in the day, if you wanted to wish the very worst upon someone and their family, you at least had to buy a stamp. You had that much invested in it, along, quite possibly, with a trip to the postbox. Now the power to offend lies in the palms of people's hands, within a couple of twitches of their thumbs. All of that steam getting let off where people can see it (and by people who might previously have thought twice about it) has not, shall we say, made the world a less fractious place.

So, something out there in the public domain that runs counter to all of that and offers a refuge from it – well, I could hardly think that was a bad idea. That show we made, back in the 1990s, was pure escapism at a time when people seemed to need it. And if people needed it then, my sense is that people need it even more now.

I would say that, of all the parts in that lovely show, the hardest to fill will be that of Mariette. The quality that was found in Catherine Zeta-Jones will be hard to find again. She had that rare and indefinable commodity: 'the camera loved her', as they say. And the viewers followed suit.

Nevertheless, a new version of *Darling Buds*? Consider me entirely in favour. Help yourself, Bradley. Fill your boots, son.

By the way, if there's a cameo role in need of filling ...

CHAPTER ELEVEN

On ending things the right way, keeping things going, and staying on the right side of the law

DS Annie Marsh: *'You can't win them all, not every case.'*
Frost: *'I can try.'* (A Touch of Frost)

A while ago I had dinner with my friend the actor Johnny Lyons. Johnny played George Toolan in *A Touch of Frost*, and our conversation inevitably turned back to those good old days of solving crimes and arresting people in the Denton area.

'I miss *Frost*,' Johnny said.

'So do I,' I said.

'Couldn't we do another series?' he said.

I thought about this for a moment.

'No,' I replied.

'Why not?' said Johnny.

'Because I'm too old,' I said. 'And you're dead.'

True, that. In the final, wrenching twist at the end of the series, after forty-two feature-length episodes across eighteen years, poor old Detective Sergeant Toolan was knocked off outside the church where Frost had just arrived to marry Christine Moorhead, played by Phyllis Logan.

Sitting nearby in a Land Rover Discovery, Christine's drunken ex-husband was seen drawing deeply on a silver flask. Then, maddened by jealousy and liquor, he drove straight into the side of the groom's car outside the church with a view to spoiling my big day and bringing the distinguished career of Detective Inspector William Edward 'Jack' Frost to an unfortunate close after fifteen series.

Cue some moments of confusion and edge-of-the-seat national anxiety as we rushed with Christine to the hospital, in an agonising state of unknowing, only to discover that it was the entirely innocent Johnny Lyons who had suffered most grievously in that murderous assault.

It could so easily have been me. In fact, it *was* me in one of the two alternative versions of the ending that were filmed. ITV, at this monumental moment for the future of the television detective genre, was keen that we should keep all the balls in the air until the very last minute – hence three separate endings, only one of which would be broadcast.

So, in one telling of the story, the groom's car gets bashed, we rush again, in a state of suspenseful unknowing, to the hospital, where I am dazed but apparently fine following that nasty smash, and where I am all set to undergo a minor precautionary check-up. But then (big plot twist) it all becomes too much for me on that hospital trolley and I go into cardiac arrest. (Some of my finest wordless acting there, dear reader, and yet bound for the cutting-room floor. How often one's thespian candle is destined to burn unnoticed.)

Phyllis Logan, my poor fiancée, finds herself watching as my life support machine is switched off. And on her wedding day and everything. And no doubt it will have been scant consolation to her that her ex-husband also perished in this ultimately suicidal act of revenge. But, of course, she will eventually go on to land a big part in *Downton Abbey*, so don't feel too sorry for her.

I am then given a funeral with full police honours. Which I suppose would have been something. No part in *Downton Abbey*, though. What do I have to do?

Then there was the second alternate version. In that one, me and Johnny Lyons got off relatively lightly with a couple of cuts and a broken arm between us, and it was Bruce Alexander as Superintendent Stanley Mullett, Frost's jousting partner on so many occasions, who ended up reaching an unlooked-for conclusion.

The neat thing was, in the event of either Toolan or Mullett being the chosen victim, Frost could still decide that police work no longer lured him as once it had, and that the office simply wouldn't be the same from this moment on.

(These days we have global pandemics to put people off working in offices. Back then it was a far more complicated matter.)

And then, in the episode's closing scenes, I could elect to leave the job behind, pledge myself eternally to Christine, and in a manner both mournful and optimistic, head off down a leafy lane and into the marital sunset.

Assuming, of course, that ITV went with that version rather than the one in which I conked out. Frost conking out would mean he wouldn't be going into the office any-time soon in any case. Nor heading down any leafy lanes and into any marital sunsets, either.

Nobody knew which version of the story would be screened. Viewers were teasingly promised a shock ending, but with no further elaboration. It was all a closely guarded secret in order to protect the drama of the moment as tightly as possible.

However, I was at least asked for my opinion about which ending should go out, and, in a move that possibly won't surprise you, I voted against the one in which Frost died.

'Well, why would a turkey vote for Christmas?' you might reasonably be thinking, but I would argue that there was a little more to it than looking after number one.

Yes, if Frost had been bumped off, it would have com-pletely ruled out the possibility of anyone ever plausibly bringing him back to the screen. Not, at any rate, without one of those 'but it was only a dream' switches, which might have been all right for American shows like *Dallas* but which British television largely has the good sense to turn up its nose at.

But no more work for Frost wouldn't necessarily have worried me at the time. This was 2010 and I was seventy, or 'three score and ten', as we say at the bingo. Now, I was a startlingly flexible and sparkly-eyed three score and ten, it goes without saying. Yet the chief reason for bringing the curtain down on the show was that it was getting less and less plausible that someone of my, shall we say, advancing maturity would have found continuing work with the police force.

In the real world, they tend to heave out the detective inspectors at sixty, in fact, before they start going upstairs to the crime scene and then wondering why they did so. Or before they start forgetting who they've interviewed and who they haven't. Or before they start putting down the keys to the interrogation room and then ... but you get the picture. Consequently, even if it certainly wasn't time for me to retire as an actor (perish the thought), it was definitely time for Frost to retire as a detective.

On the other hand, not all that long ago I was hearing an idea for a new series in which Frost, after a decade with his feet up in a quiet bungalow on the Isle of Wight, is teased out of his armchair and persuaded to use his wisdom and expertise to help out a young and aspiring private detective – possibly his daughter, in one rendering of the tale. That proposal and some very similar ones have flitted across my in-tray a couple of times recently. Nothing concrete has come of any of it at the time of writing, but maybe there's some potential there.

Also, a few nice location shoots on the Isle of Wight? Point me at it.

One thing was for sure, though: we wouldn't even be having the conversation if Frost had been allowed to slip away on that hospital trolley in 2010. Clearly you need to be as careful as you can be about bumping off a lead character because, as sound an idea as it might seem at the time, you have no way of knowing how the winds might blow in the ensuing years, and whether you'll end up finding another use for him.

The lesson being: staying alive has as much in its favour now as it did when the Bee Gees first recommended it in 1977.

But the main reason for protecting Frost at the very end, it seemed to me, was that it would have been just too much of a low blow, narrative-wise, for the series to go out on. Consider the arrangement: Frost had finally found love again, late in life, with Christine. He was about to be married, for heaven's sake. The show had brought him to this potentially contented point and, for the viewer, it would have been a highly comforting place to leave him.

You had seen him in the car with Toolan, setting out from home for the church on the morning of the wedding, when a drunken and raging ex-husband was the last thing on his mind, and when he had finally been able to pronounce himself, after much Frost-like reflection, a happy person – not something that had been on the cards all that frequently in the series for this often dispirited man with a heavy weight of sadness (the death after a long illness of his wife) in his recent past.

If you wanted to thread some emotional trauma through that final scenario, then you could possibly do so, it seemed to me, by engineering the loss of another character. But pulling the rug from under Frost himself … well, I would have found that too much to take as a viewer, quite apart from as the actor playing Frost.

So when I say I was relieved to watch that final episode on the night of broadcast and see that it was Johnny Lyons who copped it rather than me, I mean that in the nicest possible way, and with thoughts for what was best for the show and its audience uppermost in my mind. Poor old Johnny had been working in the theatre that night, so he didn't know he was dead until he came home to find his wife in tears. Acting can be cruel like that.

Johnny Lyons, incidentally, is another one of those people I met in the business with whom I turned out to have a lot in common. Like me, he was born in London during the war. Like me, he grew up in a working-class household that had to make ends meet. His mum was a cleaner, like mine, and his dad was an East End docker. He left school, as I did, at fifteen with the best part of less than nothing in the way of qualifications and, like me, took a manual job – in his case, as a labourer for British Rail at Paddington Station. One day somebody handed him a flyer for a new drama school and he went and auditioned. He paid his own way through that school by doing an evening job and then made his way into the theatre from there.

Johnny jokingly refers to me as his 'little white knight' because *Frost* came along at just the right time for him. He had started a printing business to supplement his acting work and a few unscrupulous clients had left him in the lurch. That regular work helped him out of a hole. I think of friends like Johnny when people are casually wheeling out the old stereotype of actors as airy types with no feet in the real world. Maybe some are. I know a lot who aren't.

Frost came along at a good time for me, as well – a big and entirely different kind of role to follow Pa Larkin and set me on a wholly new path. And no intimations of tax dodging in the character's background for once. I really was beginning to acquire range, it seemed.

On the other hand, Frost was quite the rule-bender, of course, as was nicely established in that early scene when he bumps a car in the police station car park and then, with a surreptitious look around, quickly sweeps away the evidence of the broken reflector with his foot before heading on into work. So maybe I was still being typecast for my seemingly effortless ability to convey borderline criminality, even at this stage in the game.

Never mind. The show came up as the consequence of a meeting I had with the bigwigs at Yorkshire Television in the wake of *Darling Buds*. It was a meeting in which, I guess, I had been expecting to hear about a part they had in mind for me or some specific project that was out there that they would like me to consider. Instead of that, though, I was asked the question, 'What would you like to do next?'

I couldn't believe my ears. 'What would I like to do? What – you're giving me carte blanche to *pick* something?'

I remember a girlfriend in my youth, to whom I had possibly divulged my dreams of actorly greatness, asking me, perhaps a little sceptically, what would be my definition of success – what would be the sign that told me I had finally 'made it'.

My answer: it would be the moment I was able to walk into a car dealership and buy a red E-Type Jag with white upholstery. That was where the pinnacle stood, according to my young man's mind: having enough money to buy a frivolous but exciting car, the ownership of which, as I saw it, would confirm my arrival among the special people.

What can I say? I was young. And, in my defence, the E-Type Jag was a very nice car, especially in red. Nevertheless, I had obviously fallen into the classic mistake there of assuming that success meant material acquisitions. Well, I never did get to buy that car, so I don't know what that might have felt like. But what I can vividly recall is the feeling I had when I started out as an actor, and when I was firing off applications in response to small ads at the back of *The Stage* – that agitated mixture of hope and anxiety and, frequently, desperation, just praying that something, somewhere would come good. (*The Stage* was the actors' recruitment bible, although I'm not sure the likes of Tom Cruise ever found themselves browsing there for a possible job.)

And now, all that work later, the day had come when, utterly unthinkably, I was being asked what I wanted to do next. It was a question that literally nobody in broadcasting had ever asked me before. So I'll need to correct my youthful self, then. Rather than any trip to the car showroom, that meeting with Yorkshire Television was the point where it occurred to me to wonder whether I might actually, after all this time, have made it.

And what I wanted to do next, seeing as I was being asked, was become a detective at the age of fifty-two. And what do you know? It turned out, through the mystical and time-honoured alchemy of showbusiness, that I could. The police force stipulates that you need to be five foot seven to join up. But if you're an actor, you can be five foot six and nobody bats an eyelid – not if you stand up straight, at any rate, and try not to spend too much time on camera standing close to the properly tall people.

You can also go straight in as a detective without having to work your way up through the ranks – although I had been a copper with Terry Scott in panto that time, so you can't say I didn't have any experience on the beat.

I'd seen a bit of life on the other side of the thin blue line, too, now I come to think of it. For I had played a part in *Softly, Softly*, one of the earliest British police procedural shows. Indeed, falling in February 1966, it must be accounted my first appearance on television in a dramatic capacity – excluding the previous year's swinging policemen, obviously, which was dramatic but in another sense.

Blink and you would have missed me in *Softly, Softly*, though. In a scene which brought me nowhere near the star of the show, the great Stratford Johns, I played a character called Smith, an implausibly named criminal accomplice who had no words to say for himself, but merely had to be seen, very briefly, fast asleep in a parked van, prior to getting woken up by a policeman's torch, shone in inquisitively from the pavement.

A small part, then, and yet once again we must return to one of this book's most important mottoes and perhaps its most crucial take-away: no small parts, only small actors. And five foot six is quite small enough. I invested everything into that moment in the literal spotlight that my inexperienced, work-hungry 26-year-old self could muster. I didn't just sleep in the front of that van: I *slept*, properly, profoundly, from the bottom of my soul. And when the beam from that policeman's torch hit my slumbering face, I shot to alertness with a speed and vigour that was later confirmed to have broken all existing records for getting woken up in a van by a policeman. And then I went home, with the warm satisfaction of a person who has not just done his job, but done his job well.

Reader, I overcooked it. Frankly, I was embarrassed when I saw it back. My acting at that point was so hammy you could have sliced it thickly and served it with pickle in one of Ma Larkin's sandwiches. If I had burst into song upon waking and given them a verse of 'Somewhere Over the Rainbow', it couldn't have looked any more overdone. I guess eighteen years in a starring role in this kind of programme seemed a long way off at that point – and, indeed, it *was* a long way off. But from humble beginnings, and all that.

The lesson being: try not to give 110 per cent when 100 per cent will do.

I'm not sure the people at Yorkshire Television in that meeting expected me to say I fancied becoming a copper. Indeed, I seem to recall a few startled faces around the table. They were probably thinking I would propose something more in the straight comedy line. Let's be honest, poking around in disused quarries for evidence of murders wasn't something that I'd been doing much of up to now. But of course, once again, that was the point as far as I was concerned – to seek out something different. I wanted to be an actor to take on different roles, be different people and, at the same time, conceal myself. Just playing safe or always playing comedy was not what I joined up for.

And they took me seriously. They looked into some possibilities for development and they sent me a stack of detective novels to consider, which I took on holiday with me. And the one I liked the most and felt I could get something out of was R. D. Wingfield's *A Touch of Frost*.

It was dark and modern and, as such, a long way from H. E. Bates territory, which was obviously important to me at the time, and at its centre was this slightly shabby, dry and cynical but ultimately extremely human and relatable character, an exhausted workaholic with little patience for red tape and a predilection for junk food at the wrong times of the day. It wasn't long after reading it that I was on the phone to David Reynolds, saying, 'If you get me *Frost*, I'll do it ... ' I came back from that holiday and waited for them to do all the legal stuff around acquiring the rights. It was touch and go for a while and that made me realise even more how much I wanted the challenge.

And the rest, as they say, is closed cases. All forty-two of them. Happy days, indeed. I know how fortunate I was to land up working with the crew on that show: terrific, easy-going actors who were fun to be around, crack writers who really knew what they were about, including Richard

Harris, Christopher Russell and Malcolm Bradbury, and great directors such as Don Leaver, Roger Bamford, Adrian Shergold and of course Paul Harrison, who went on to become a good friend.

I remember the shadow of mild discontent falling over our happy ship just once in all those years. It was when Herbie Wise came in to direct an episode in series three in 1995. All respect was due to Herbie, who had an amazing CV, including directing *I, Claudius* and various Shakespeare adaptations for television. But he was very much of the 'I tell you what to do and you get on and do it' school of directing, which I hadn't much come across before. I seemed to have been lucky enough to work with directors who looked for input from their teams and encouraged a bit of back-and-forth. But that wasn't Herbie's style. He turned up every day with everything planned and plotted and everyone was expected to slot in accordingly. It made for a very efficient shoot, but perhaps not a particularly relaxed one.

Herbie, incidentally, had also worked on *Inspector Morse* and made the unfortunate mistake one day, while asking me to move to a certain place on the set, of calling me 'Mr Morse'.

Oops, wrong show.

I didn't mind that so much – he could have called me Miss Marple, for all I really cared and for all it really mattered. What I did object to was something Herbie was overheard muttering to his first assistant one day: 'The trouble with David Jason is he thinks he's part of the creative process.'

Well, pardon me for my presumption. But I actually *do* think actors are part of the creative process. I happen to think the props person is part of the creative process. Everybody in the production is part of the creative process. I guess Herbie and I just had very different approaches. Still, not to worry. It was a good episode, even so, although I did have to bite my tongue on a number of occasions.

Frost turned out to be another of those characters to whom audiences felt able to form an attachment and who continues to mean something to people, even though his journey is concluded. And exactly how much he means was made graphically apparent when, at the end of summer in 2020, ITV invited the public to vote for its favourite TV detective and screened the results in a two-hour bank holiday special, counting down from twenty-five. And in that all-important vote, I can blushingly report that Frost finished ...

Twelfth?

Only *twelfth?*

Well, naturally, my first instinct was to write directly to the returning officer and demand a recount. Because this couldn't be right, could it? I'm not sure exactly how the voting worked, but this was one of those poll-based television run-down shows, so I'm sure it was scientifically rigorous, with a strict 'one person, one vote' system in place and with independent scrutiny of the electoral process at every stage. Aren't they always? Yet somehow, something seemed to have gone badly awry in this instance.

Twelfth!

But then I took a moment for some tranquil reflection – never a bad idea. And actually, twelfth wasn't too shabby, was it? OK, a top ten finish would have been nice. But twelfth out of twenty-five could hardly be accounted a disgrace, and certainly not when you considered the quality of the field.

I mean, cast your eyes over the contenders. I'll have you know, a lot of crime-fighting heavyweights fell by the wayside before we got down as far as twelve. *Taggart?* Brushed aside much earlier – all 110 episodes of him. *Rebus?* Another big-hitter left in the dust. *Frost* was even deemed too strong at the end of the day for *Cagney and Lacey* – and there were two of them, so it was hardly a fair fight.

Tom Selleck as *Magnum, PI?* No match for Frost on this occasion. He was beaten back, and not even the presence of Orson Welles in that classic US eighties series could save him. (Orson, you may recall, provided the voice of the retired author, never seen, on whose magnificent Hawaiian estate Magnum had his home. It was good to know, I guess, that Orson continued to find paying work despite those busker-interrupted appearances at Newcastle's Theatre Royal.)

Also forced to admit defeat and stand aside were Robbie Coltrane's Fitz from *Cracker*, Kevin Whately as Lewis, Alan Davies as Jonathan Creek, and (blimey, this was a really big one) Dame Helen Mirren's DCI Tennison in *Prime Suspect*, which was one of my favourites.

Great series and great actors all, of course, but I suppose unfortunately they had just come up against the fourth hardest-working man in showbusiness, and clearly the power and pace at this level were simply too much for them.

Then consider the mighty figures in the crime-busting game who, for whatever reason, polled higher than *Frost*. Again, in this company, shame in defeat could hardly enter the equation. There was DCI John Luther, for example, as played by Idris Elba. We've got a lot of time for *Luther* round my way. There were both the Agatha Christie greats – Miss Marple and Hercule Poirot – and Angela Lansbury from *Murder, She Wrote*. No arguments there: those three had some serious history on their side.

And there was John Nettles as Tom Barnaby in *Midsomer Murders* and let's face it, of all the people on this list, he really had to put a shift in. The murderous inclinations of the people of the county of Midsomer were famously un-rivalled, to the point where John was handling an average of 2.6 murders per episode at the peak of his powers. Ask anyone who has appeared in a detective series: that's an astonishing work rate and worthy of a high place on any roll of honour.

And there was Morse. No way was I picking a fight with Morse. It was watching and enjoying *Inspector Morse* that made me want to do a detective show in the first place. And it was watching John Thaw successfully make that transition from tough, scrappy cockney Flying Squad geezer in *The Sweeney* to the cerebral, Oxford-based, classical music-loving mystery-solver that emboldened me to think that I might have a chance at it.

Number one and the nation's favourite this time? Sherlock Holmes. Again, fair enough. No complaints from me. Everyone who does fictional police work operates to some extent in the shadow of Conan Doyle's great pipe-smoking creation, and presumably we always will do.

So, twelfth: I'll take that. And there's always next year (or whenever they run one of these polls again).

Interestingly, Robbie Coltrane, who so memorably played Fitz in *Cracker*, talked in that ITV show about the appeal of a detective series for an actor and pointed out that it was in the police interview sequences that you could really get to show what you can do. He was right about that. When there was an interview room scene in the script, I would be rubbing my hands with glee and getting ready to get stuck in. It was something about the very basic nature of the set-up – a two-person dialogue, normally, with the bare minimum in the way of props and furnishings, and with rudimentary lighting, even. The whole scene would be dependent on words and faces. It was a unique opportunity to show off your chops.

Funnily enough, I already knew that to be true about interrogation scenes from *Only Fools and Horses*, albeit from the other side of the table. You might remember the episode from series three – 'May the Force Be with You' – where Del ends up at the police station getting interrogated by DCI Slater, brilliantly embodied by Jim Broadbent.

Del's crime: the handling of a stolen microwave. But Slater will let Del off that misdemeanour and permit him to walk free if he turns copper's nark and shops the actual thief. Del, of course (I believe I am obliged to bellow the words 'SPOILER ALERT' at this point, just in case you haven't seen this legendary piece of work and intend to) eventually snookers Slater by saying, 'It was me.'

In the meantime, though, we've been treated to a long and inch-perfect pastiche of the typical police procedural interview scene, with me and Jim knocking the lines backwards and forwards and with Del seeming to go through absolute agonies with his conscience at the prospect of having no choice but to become a grass.

It was another of those moments where *Only Fools* was able to exceed its 'sitcom' brief and expand into wholly other areas of character and action, only to pull it out of the fire with the big punchline at the end. Little did I know at the time how many hours I would be spending in police interrogation rooms further down the line.

When *Frost* eventually came to an end, there was a press conference to announce the news. Imagine being in a show that grows so big in the public's estimation that you have to throw a press conference in order to inform the media of breaking developments regarding the leading character. That seemed to me to be a case of art and life getting rather too closely bundled up, but you couldn't help but feel astounded and flattered by it.

At the conference, I said a few words about Frost getting a bit long in the tooth and suggested that it was probably time to decide that enough was enough. 'You wouldn't want me to play Frost in a wheelchair,' I added.

Hang on, though: there's an idea there. A cop in a wheelchair ... Has anyone ever done that?

What's that? *Ironside?* With Raymond Burr? Sounds like a bloke who's been out in the cold all night.

It'll never work. Then again, if it does, I'm available.

CHAPTER TWELVE

On learning from the best, on taking stock, and on getting back out there

And so, dear reader, we close in gradually on the end of this volume. As a carpet dealer in a far-flung souk once said to me, while I was bartering with him for a rug: 'The elephant has gone through the eye of a needle, only his tail remains.'

Or, in other words, the deal is nearly done: raise your price by a couple more quid and the goods are yours. (It stayed with me, that carpet dealer's expression. I've used it ever since about jobs that are nearly complete.)

As I write, the summer of this unprecedented year is ending. Through the mullioned window of my book-lined library the evening sun spreads its lengthening shadows, the rooks return to their nests in the coppice, and Strobes, my wrinkled retainer, climbs on his bike and sets off unsteadily up the drive for his humble home after completing another sixteen-hour shift.

I must have a word with him about that. I've told him before about only using the back gate.

Meanwhile, the flag bearing my coat of arms atop the turret on the east wing – the traditional signal to a hopefully comforted nation that I am presently in residence – stirs gently in a wind that brings a new chill with it, clearly presaging autumn.

OK, all day dreams again, of course. Apart from the bit about autumn. And actually, now I come to mention it, I do have a coat of arms, although not on a flag – behind glass, in a framed certificate.

Obviously being a knight of the realm (an honour bestowed upon me in 2005 for services to acting, in case I haven't mentioned this yet) comes with its perks. Automatic upgrades on aeroplanes, the best rooms in hotels and triple Nectar points – not so much. More day dreams, I'm afraid, but you do get invited to choose yourself a coat of arms.

You apply to the Somerset Herald (not a newspaper, an officer appointed by Her Majesty) at the College of Arms in Queen Victoria Street in London. And then you make an appointment, and go along to the aforementioned college, where the extremely helpful staff take down a giant portfolio of existing designs, beautifully rendered in coloured ink, for you to thumb through. It's a tome containing all of the Coats of Arms right back to the very beginning. They then help you to come up with one of your own.

Along the way, as I thumbed, there were some entirely blank pages.

'What are those?' I mildly enquired.

Apparently they were the shields of those knights who, for misdemeanours unspecified, had had their knighthoods, and therefore their coats of arms, stripped from them and removed from the record.

I gulped. There were standards to be kept up here, clearly. One slightly under par episode of *Still Open All Hours*, and that blank shield could be me.

However, as a consequence of that visit to the college, and at the time of writing, I am the proud bearer (or, at least my wall is) of the Sir David John White coat of arms, the official and wonderfully archaic, not to mention bravely unpunctuated, heraldic description of which, as it appears on the certificate, is as follows:

Per fess wavy Ore and Azure in chief a Mask of Comedy and a Mask of Tragedy Azure attached thereto ribbons Gules and in base a Propeller of three blades in front of three Lightning Flashes in pairle Ore.

Try saying that with a mouthful of wine gums. But what it essentially means is that the shield is divided horizontally in two by a wavy line ('Per fess wavy'), that the backgrounds of the two parts are gold and blue ('Ore and Azure'), and that the top half shows a traditional pair of dramatic masks, with reference to my job and with red ribbons trailing from them ('ribbons Gules'), while the bottom part has a golden propeller surrounded by three lightning flashes, which I chose to denote my interest in flying and my past as an electrician.

That's it, then. That's the shield I'll be carrying on the battlefield the next time there's a civil war, so now you can spot me out there. Come over and say hello, won't you? As long as we're on the same side, of course, which I'm sure we would be.

I also had to provide, for my shield, a motto in Latin which, with any luck, would go some way towards summing up my philosophy, or at any rate my approach to my business, in an uplifting and inspiring manner. So, along the bottom of my crest are emblazoned these two words: *conata perficere*.

No, it's not a song from *The Lion King*. I think you may be thinking of 'Hakuna Matata', and I wouldn't have been allowed to have that because a) it's not Latin and b) it's copyright. No, in point of fact I drew on my extensive readings of the writings of Julius Caesar in their original Latin, and particularly his account of the Gallic Wars, which are my favourites – yours too, I have no doubt – and I settled (OK, with a little bit of help and prompting) on those two words: *conata perficere*.

Which is to say, to accomplish one's enterprises, to reach one's goals – as I like to point out to my long-suffering daughter, 'to achieve what one attempts.'

The lesson being: *conata perficere*. And you'll know what that means now.

Not that I'm bragging, but I have a room at home that serves to remind me, when I need reminding, that I did, indeed, *perficere* a few *conatas*. It's the room I'm working in right now, in fact. On the mantelpiece, there are four Baftas. Dotted around elsewhere, there are eight National Television Awards, three British Comedy awards, three Sony radio awards, several *Radio Times* awards, several *TV Times* awards … Quite a lot of those honours were for making people laugh, so it's hardly any wonder that I occasionally shake my head and remember the words of the legendary Jerry Lewis: 'I've had great success being a total idiot.'

Sitting among the trophies is the medal I was given when I received the OBE, and, somewhere else, the medal I received when I was appointed to the Order of Knight's Bachelor – or made a 'sir', if you prefer to think of it that way. That second medal in particular is worth a lot to me. Indeed, if I show it at the checkout, I get 20 per cent off armour, plus free admission to see The Bachelors if ever they reform.

Seriously, though, never in my wildest imaginings did I dream of accumulating such bounty. Remember, I originally gave myself just five years at this lark. If I hadn't got anywhere by the age of thirty, I was giving it up and going back to the day job.

I'm quite glad I persisted.

Of course, there's one little statuette missing from my collection: an Oscar. It was cinema that first put the idea of acting in my head, and I guess that there was always some small part of me that was hoping acting would eventually lead me back there – but facing the other way this time, the figure on the screen looking out, as all those figures had looked out at me as I perched there in awe on my tipped-up seat.

Alas, somehow those major film roles just kept on failing to materialise. That might have caused me to chew on my lip for a while. It can be a strong temptation, of course, to latch on to the thing you didn't manage to achieve rather than draw satisfaction from all the things that you did. But not any more. One of the advantages of age is that I can take the longer view. I did OK.

And besides, who says the chance has gone? My phone is where it always was, should Hollywood now wish to call.

The lesson being: don't be bound by your circumstances. Extraordinary things happen to ordinary people.

'Look, mark, learn, inwardly digest': a Latin translation of those five words might have served me as a motto for my trusty shield if Julius Caesar hadn't stepped in. 'Look, mark, learn, inwardly digest' was the little mantra that I repeated to myself constantly back in those early days, when I was beginning to find myself alongside established names in the business and, in need of guidance myself, observing their methods of doing things, the way they approached their work and the people around them, their behaviour on the set – good and bad.

Be lucky in your teachers, they say, and, as I hope this book has shown, I was exceptionally lucky in mine, and not least of all in landing up alongside Ronnie Barker. I've saved the biggest mentor of them all until last here, because it was around Ronnie B that I did most of my best looking, marking, learning and inwardly digesting. Looking back over my life this time has only made me appreciate still more clearly how fortunate I was to be in a position to benefit from his influence.

A few months after I had played Dithers, the hundred-year-old gardener whom we talked about right back at the beginning of this book, Ronnie rang me and asked if I would be interested in acting with him in a two-hander called *The Odd Job*. This was for a series of one-off, half-hour television plays under the heading *Six Dates with Barker*. I loved the script, by Bernard McKenna, which was about a man whose wife (Joan Sims) leaves him and who then, in a state of abject misery, tries and fails, in a variety of comical ways, to commit suicide.

Right on cue, an odd job man comes to the door, looking for work.

Ronnie was going to play the suicidal husband and he wanted me to play the odd job man. On reflection, I was quite naïve about it. Having read the script, I rang the producer, Humphrey Barclay, and said, 'This character you want me to play – he's got all the funny lines. Are you sure that's not the role that Ronnie wants to be playing?' But that was my earliest lesson about what Ronnie was like. It wasn't about who got the laughs – he couldn't have cared less. There was no greed for glory in the man. It was about the overall effect of the piece, and what worked best.

There is one piece of comic timing in that show of which I remain particularly proud. It follows a conversation between our characters in which we're discussing what might be the best time for the odd job man to do the deed and bump Ronnie's character off. And my character explains that, obviously an element of surprise would be important and that he would probably be inclined to do the job at the moment when it's least expected.

There is then a short silence, while Ronnie's character digests this. Then, as Ronnie says, 'Well, I suppose … ' – blam! I go straight for his throat and we start having a vigorous fight on the sofa.

It's about two bits of timing, really: it's the space that Ronnie carefully measures out, as he sits and thinks, and it's the point at which I jump him and interrupt him when he starts speaking again. And it's the fact that nothing about either of our body positions gives away the comic physical violence which is about to kick off. All of this was meticulously planned and rehearsed by Ronnie, and watching how he put it together and his attention to detail was an absolute revelation to me. Like so much that Ronnie did, it steered me towards a path.

There's a line in *The Odd Job* that my character says to Ronnie's: 'Lucky we met, isn't it?' Indeed it was. We were quickly good friends. I spent a lot of time at Ronnie's house, with him and his wife, Joy, and their kids, Larry, Adam and Charlotte. What you soon found out was that Ronnie on the set was the same as Ronnie off the set. He was himself in any circumstance. I admired him for that. He was at ease with himself in a way that was somehow a lifetime away from arrogance. He was eleven years older than me but our journeys into the business had had something in common, and I think he saw a kindred spark in me that he was happy to encourage. We had both quit jobs to become actors – Ronnie had been working in a bank before he took the plunge – and we had both come up through repertory theatre and endured those typical hardships and humiliations that kept our feet on the ground forever after. (Ronnie, topping all my stories of deprivation in this area, had been in a company which actually went bust while he was out on the road, leaving him entirely cashless and meaning he actually had to spend two days walking and hitching his way home to Oxford from Penzance. A B&B with cat hair and electric sheets must have seemed a golden vision at that point.)

Ronnie was constantly verbally inventive and witty, and great company from that point of view. But it wasn't in his nature to dominate a room. He was far too shy and self-deprecating for that. In order to be funny as a public performer, he needed to find a character. This, too, we shared. He rehearsed and rehearsed – he wrote and rewrote. He was forever tinkering with scripts, trying to see if there was anything funnier that could be squeezed out of them. Ronnie Corbett once noticed that, in an entire season of shows at the London Palladium, Ronnie B worked so precisely that even his hand gestures were the same, show after show. He made it look natural, but it was anything but. It was the product of hard study.

Perhaps most important of all, he taught me respect for the fact that absolutely *everybody* involved in a show contributes to that show's success. On the shows I witnessed where Ronnie was the star (*Hark at Barker*, *His Lordship Entertains*, *Porridge*, *Open All Hours*), I saw how, with him, it worked like a pyramid: at the tip was the leading actor – in his case, talented, funny, considerate, sharing, wonderfully ego-free – and he spread those things all the way down. It was the most productive way to work, and the most fun, too. I looked, marked, learned, inwardly digested.

In 2003, two years before he died at the age of seventy-six, Ronnie came to the London Palladium to give the speech and make the presentation of my BAFTA Fellowship Award. He shied away from that kind of thing, but he did it for me. And, of course, he was funny, not least when foxed by a little slip of the autocue: 'In my option ... I don't have an option actually. Actually what I have is an opinion. It's because I belong to the Lord's Society of Pissmonunciation ...'

When he called my name, I remember rising out of my seat beside Gill to head for the stage in front of that audience, so intimidatingly packed with the great and the good – Sir David Attenborough, Vanessa Redgrave, Albert Finney, Kenneth Branagh ... I had felt pretty calm throughout the evening, knowing the award was going to be made. (They don't surprise you with a Bafta Fellowship. It's the highest honour that the academy can bestow, an acknowledgement of 'outstanding achievement in the art forms of the moving image'. They have the decency to let you know you're getting one in advance.) But now, at the actual moment, something about the circumstances and the scale of it all and what it said about the journey I had taken across all those years and the fact that it was Ronnie up there about to bestow this extraordinary endorsement ... all of those things at once hit home.

Even as I headed up the theatre aisle, I was becoming a jelly and my carefully rehearsed acceptance speech was melting out of my head like butter in a frying pan. I would end up shakily gibbering a few thank yous. But in the meantime I made it to the podium where Ronnie gave me this huge bear hug and all I could think to say to him was, 'Who'd have thought it, eh?'

That was the summit, I now realise. All the way from Friern Barnet's Incognito Theatre to there, and not so incognito any more it seemed. And what a climb. Higher than I had ever imagined possible. Who'd have thought it, indeed.

During lockdown in 2020, it was possible sometimes to experience a tranquillity of a kind that maybe very few of us had previously known in the course of our ordinary lives. I had the feeling that, even in the very worst of it, communities were quietly pulling together, whether in cities, towns or the countryside. Little units formed around us all, if we were lucky, and we probably felt the camaraderie and support that smaller communities experienced decades ago. It was probably the thing that got many of us through the shock and worry at the start of it all.

However, a little tranquillity goes a long way, I tend to find. There came a point during those months where I ran out of things to do. I had finally fixed that downlighter which was out in the bathroom – braving, I should say, the attendant indignity because every time you take something down from the ceiling in our house, a shower of powdered cork from the insulation descends into your face, as if there is somebody up there shovelling it down on you. Could it be a little elf lives up there?

Anyway, I'd dealt with that. (A burnt-out unit, thanks for asking. I replaced it.) Then I'd moved on to that loose door handle, taking it to pieces and re-assembling it. Except (the law of sod applying here, as it so often does), when I'd finished the door no longer shut properly because the new latch was too big for the strike plate. So it was back out to the workshop to fetch the files, before I eventually realised that what I really needed, of course, was the Dremel. So that was another trip out to the workshop. And then I had to go back out there again because I needed the screwdriver – and then to return yet again because it was the slotted one that I needed … But I guess it filled some time. (I could get someone in to do these kinds of jobs, I suppose. But because I can do it, and I know how to do it, and I'm brought up to think you should do it, I do it myself.)

Similarly, I had finished putting some decking in around the pond, which also ate up a few days. I had written most of this book. I had spent a morning seeing how much cockney rhyming slang I could remember and squeeze into one paragraph (see Appendix). I had re-read *Under Milk Wood*, the Dylan Thomas piece which I have helped voice in various ways in various forms down the years, and which I always find a comfort and a steady companion – especially the words given to the Reverend Eli Jenkins, whom I particularly enjoyed playing. Look them up if you don't know them. They are a joy.

But, frankly, with all that completed, I was at a loose end that wasn't getting any tighter. The noise that could be heard through our house on some of those longer afternoons was the sound of my fingers drumming on the table.

What a relief, then, in mid-July, as the restrictions slightly eased, to hear the phone ring with an offer of actual work. I fell upon it as a thirsty man in the desert falls on water – even under the terms of the 'new normal'. So, who were those two masked men, heading up the A1 and trusting their destiny once again, as in the glory days of yore, to a dodgy satnav? It was me, that's who, and my legendary driver Les Davis, whose motto ('there are drivers, and there are drivers') is one for the ages.

In PPE and suitably distanced, I was bound, as it happened, for RAF Coningsby in Lincolnshire in order to present a documentary about the Battle of Britain Memorial Flight. As I mentioned back in the introduction, just like me and Ringo the Battle of Britain was celebrating its eightieth anniversary in 2020 and I was naturally keen in any way that I could to help mark the occasion and encourage the remembrance of that pivotal event in our history.

The mission of the BBMF (to quote the RAF) is 'to maintain the priceless artefacts of our national heritage in airworthy condition in order to commemorate those who have fallen in the service of this country, to promote the modern-day Air Force and to inspire the future generations'. It is, as such, a great institution. I was shown to the hangar where a gigantic Lancaster bomber sat at one end, like a huge bird of prey looking after her brood of six Spitfires, two Hurricanes, a C-47 Dakota and two Chipmunks. Those are the aircraft that make up the Memorial Flight and I have to say that every time I have seen them display, often at the International Air Tattoo at Fairford, it has never failed to move me. And now I knew the awe of getting close to those extraordinary machines and the emotional tug of seeing inside their cockpits and attempting to imagine how their bold and selfless pilots must have felt in 1940.

I also love the fact that each of these aircraft is at least eighty years old, but all of them are tended by young serving engineers who still know how to take a piston-driven aircraft engine to bits. These are my kind of people.

I had a couple of days with the BBMF in July, learning about their work and watching the planes from the ground, and then I returned to Coningsby in August for the task of filming a Hurricane and a Spitfire from the air. The arrangement was that we would fly with the planes and get our footage from the slightly more contemporary surroundings of a Robinson R44 helicopter.

Obviously, masks were again a requirement and, what with the caps and sunglasses which we were also wearing, it's possible that we looked more like a bunch of villains off to rob a bank than a TV crew. It wasn't exactly comfortable, either, to be wrapped up in that glass cockpit on one of those properly sweltering August days.

I wouldn't have missed it for anything, though. What an experience to be in the air with those nippy fighter planes as they looped and turned and barrel-rolled and danced like ballerinas 1,500 feet above the Lincolnshire countryside. Loaded up, and with the camera fitted, our helicopter's top speed was only 100 knots, so we needed the fighters to perform their passes as slowly as they could or we would never keep up. Given that the speed at which the engines on those fighters will stall is around 120 knots, we were asking the pilots to fly at the speed at which they would normally be getting worried about falling out of the sky.

Fortunately, the supremely calm and experienced pilots – Spitfire Squadron Leader Andy G. Preece, and Fighter Pilot Squadron Leader Mark 'Disco' Discombe in the Hurricane – were impressively capable of handling this difficult manoeuvre, so I could just look out of the window and watch in awe. It was quite something to witness. And the next time anyone says, 'Hands up if you've flown in formation with a Hurricane and a Spitfire,' I can proudly raise my arm.

I returned home invigorated. Work does that for me. Life as we used to know it had begun to seem dimly possible again. A thaw seemed to be underway. Maybe, in the longer term, those encouraging signs would prove illusory. But it was time, clearly, to seize them as optimistically as possible, and to begin gathering together, in as much as I could, the various bits and pieces that had got scattered to the wind by the pandemic back in March when the world froze.

A director had been on to me about the possibility of 'lending my voice' to an American animated film. Why not? I'm sure they'll let me have it back afterwards. Someone else, meanwhile, was talking to me about a potential Christmas 'entertainment spectacular' for television, which was sounding intriguing, especially once I had established that they weren't hoping to get me to do a turn as Del.

Plus, of course, we were in the middle of trying to find some way to wrap up *Still Open All Hours*. Would it be a good idea to get Granville married off? Reader, I couldn't possibly comment. But some kind of conclusion, hopefully satisfying, shall in due course be found.

So, business as ... well, not as usual, no. Not yet. Not at the time of writing. But signs, at least, of a re-emergence. And business of some kind – that's the main thing. Because that's what keeps me going. For as the great French philosopher (and singer) Charles Aznavour once said, 'A man will never grow old if he knows what he's doing tomorrow and enjoys it.' (Charles Aznavour really did say that.)

One of my dreams when I first started out in amateur dramatics – my ideal 'tomorrow', as it were – was to play at the National Theatre. That dream is still unfulfilled, I'm afraid to say. However, in the early days of auditioning for the theatrical parts which I hoped would eventually lead me that way, I would choose a passage from John Osborne's 'Look Back in Anger', which was very new at that point. And then, to demonstrate my range, I would do a classical piece. My favourite then – and to this day – was from Shakespeare, words spoken by Brutus in the play 'Julius Caesar'. They seem quite appropriate as I wrap up here, too.

> *There is a tide in the affairs of men*
> *Which, taken at the flood, leads on to fortune;*
> *Omitted, all the voyage of their life*
> *Is bound in shallows and in miseries.*
> *On such a full sea are we now afloat*
> *And we must take the current when it serves,*
> *Or lose our ventures.*

You know what? I couldn't have put it better myself.

APPENDIX

In which the author fills some painfully vacant time during lockdown by seeing how much cockney rhyming slang he can remember and how much of it he can fit in one paragraph. With a glossary for anyone who doesn't understand this kind of rabbit (and pork = talk).

So I'm sitting there on my Jack, scratching my loaf when I think to myself, 'I haven't seen my old china Rod in a while. Maybe I'll give him a bell and see if he wants to meet up in the local rub-a-dub for a pint of pig's.' Knowing him though, he'll sting me for a large tom or a needle. But what do you know? Just then the old dog barks and who should it be but the old china himself, who says he'll meet me in about an hour in the Lousy Brown. 'Tell you what,' he adds, 'I'm a bit brassic. Can you lend me a macaroni? There'll be no problem. I can let you have a goose's if you don't trust me for it. Or,' he says, 'I can pay you back Friday when I get my greens.' 'No, it's OK,' I say. 'My treat. Look, I'll take a ball up the frog and see you in an hour. But be careful tonight: last time we were there, you got so elephant's you tried to get the Governor's trouble up the apples to show her a Bushey. If I hadn't stepped in, I could see you and the Governor having a right bull.' 'Don't worry,' says Rod. 'I'll be good as gold. Hey, that Governor: was he the one with the ugly-looking Chevy? I remember him. He wouldn't let me go for a Jimmy before we left. It all comes back to me now. I tried to ram my Oliver down his ferret.' 'Yes, that's the one,' I reply. 'But he got you in the orchestras first.' 'Anyway,' says Rod, 'I'm glad I didn't use his khazi – it didn't half pen in there as I recall. All right, I'll be on my best, but can I bring my skin with me?' 'Fine,' I say, 'but not her old pot 'cos he can't half rabbit and every time I see him he gets me in a right two and eight, what with that and him being a grasshopper and all.' 'Don't worry,' says Rod. 'I'll tell her to stay on her Todd and I'll see you in an hour. Give me time to change my Dicky and have a dig.' 'OK, in that case I'll put on my new whistle and best daisies,' I say, 'and I'll even scrub me old boat and I'll meet you there alligator.' One thought: if he's bringing his skin, I'd better clean me Hampsteads before I go. With a bit of luck, I might be able to con some Jim Skinner out of him. I fancy a nice bit of Kate and Sydney or a nice piece of Lillian, starting with some loop the loop. No idea what time I'll be home so I had better take me old nanny with me in case it gets a bit taters. Anyway, I'd better get going or I'll be getting a right kick up the old April.

If you want any help with the old rabbit and pork (which is cockney for talk), here's a little glossary:

Jack (Jones) – own
Loaf (of bread) – head
China (plate) – mate
Bell – phone call
Rub-a-dub – pub
Pig's (ear) – beer
Tom (Thumb) – rum
Needle (and pin) – gin
Dog (and bone) – phone
Lousy Brown – Rose and Crown
Brassic (lint) – skint
Macaroni – pony (£25)
Goose's (neck) – cheque
Greens (greengages) – wages
Ball (of chalk) – walk
Frog (and toad) – road
Elephant's (trunk) – drunk
Trouble (and strife) – wife
Apples (and pears) – stairs
Bushey (Park) – lark
Bull (and cow) – row
Chevy (Chase) – face
Jimmy (Riddle) – piddle
Oliver (Twist) – fist

Ferret (and stoat) – throat
Orchestras (stalls) – balls
Pen (and ink) – stink
Skin (and blister) – sister
Pot (and pan) – old man
Two and eight – state
Grasshopper – copper
Todd (Jones) – own
Dicky (Dirt) – shirt
Dig in the grave – shave
Whistle (and flute) – suit
Daisy (roots) – boots
Boat (race) – face
Alligator – later
Hampstead (Heath) – teeth
Jim Skinner – dinner
Kate and Sydney – steak and kidney
Lillian (Gish) – fish
Loop the loop – soup
Nanny goat – coat
(Po)Taters (in the mould) – cold
April (in Paris = 'Arris = Aristotle = bottle = bottle and glass) – arse
(John Sullivan told me that last one and I never quite believed it.)

ACKNOWLEDGEMENTS

For my wonderful wife, Gill, a big thank you for helping me get this book into shape and keeping the ball rolling with the publishers.

INDEX